PELICAN BOOKS

BIRD RECOGNITION

I

SEA-BIRDS and WADERS

By

JAMES FISHER

(A175)

PELICAN BOOKS

BIRD RECOGNITION

I: SEA-BIRDS & WADERS

By

JAMES FISHER

With 86 illustrations by
FISH-HAWK
77 maps, mainly compiled by
W. B. ALEXANDER
and 72 charts, compiled
by the writer

PUBLISHED BY

PENGUIN BOOKS

HARMONDSWORTH MIDDLESEX ENGLAND
245 FIFTH AVENUE NEW YORK U.S.A.

First published 1947

FOR

EDMUND

MADE AND PRINTED IN GREAT BRITAIN FOR PENGUIN BOOKS, LTD.
BY HARRISON AND SONS, LTD., PRINTERS TO H.M. THE KING,
LONDON, HAYES (MIDDX.), AND HIGH WYCOMBE

INTRODUCTION

THE object of this book, and of the two companion volumes that are to follow it (*Game birds, water-fowl and birds of prey* and *Perching and singing birds*) is not a single one. It is my belief that the thousands of bird watchers in Britain today (less than a dozen of whom are professionals) want a pocket-book that enables them to recognize not only a bird's *kind*, but also its *place in nature*, and its *general importance*. A disrespectful friend of mine, when I once showed him a spotted redshank in September on a Midland sewage farm, said " So what ? " Which is a perfectly reasonable observation. This book is an attempt to answer it, not only for the spotted redshank but for all the species of waders and seabirds that have been observed more than a hundred times in Britain.

I have had a tremendous advantage over all previous compilers of similar books. By 1941, when I first began to collect my notes, the fifth and final volume of *The Handbook of British Birds*, under the general editorship of the late H. F. Witherby, had been published. This great storehouse of information, which has no parallel in any other country in the world, has been my continual guide. Particularly useful have been the sections compiled by B. W. Tucker, on habitat, field-characters and general habits, voice and display.

I must particularly thank " Fish-Hawk," not only for his pictures, but for his patience. W. B. Alexander's maps represent literally years of work, and I am grateful indeed for the opportunity to publish them. Others, to whom I have shown the book at its various stages, and who have been very helpful, include A. W. Boyd, H. Munro Fox and Julian Huxley.

Within the sea-birds and waders, I have arranged the birds in strict systematic order, by species. I have dealt with subspecies under the species to which they belong. The Witherby, or W numbers, attached to each species at the bottom of the page, correspond with those in the check-list in the *Handbook*, which is accepted as the standard list of British birds.

The two words in italics after the English name of each species form its Linnean or scientific name. The first (which always bears a capital letter) is the name of the genus and the second (which starts with a small letter) is an adjective describing it. The two together constitute the name of the species. The name in capital letters after the specific name is that of the author who first published a description of the species, and the date is the year in which he did so; if he assigned it then to a genus other than that in which it is now placed, his name is (by rule) enclosed in brackets.

At the risk of repetition I must make something quite clear:— The task of compiling this volume would have been very much greater and the information contained in it would have been very much less, had not this new standard work, *The Handbook of British Birds*, been published. It deals in immense detail with all the birds on the British list, and is illustrated in colour throughout. Its principal editor was the late Mr. H. F. Witherby and is now Mr. B. W. Tucker, who has recently revised it. It is published by Messrs. H. F. & G. Witherby, Ltd., and is in five volumes.

BOOKS ON BIRD RECOGNITION

T. A. Coward (1920 and subsequent editions). *The birds of the British Isles and their eggs*. London, Warne, Wayside and Woodland series. Entirely illustrated with the colour plates by Thorburn and Keulemans from Lord Lilford's *Coloured figures of the birds of the British Islands*. Highly recommended.

Edmund Sandars (1927 and subsequent editions). *A bird book for the pocket*. London, Oxford University Press. Crude coloured pictures. Practical and common-sensical. Recommended.

Norman H. Joy (1936 and subsequent edition). *How to know British birds*. London, Witherby. Black and white and coloured sketches. Extremely practical. Recommended.

H. F. Witherby (editor), F. C. R. Jourdain, N. F. Ticehurst and B. W. Tucker (1938–41 and subsequent edition). *The handbook of British birds*. London, Witherby, 5 vols. Coloured pictures of most stages of plumage of every species on the British list. Standard textbook. Serious students ignore it at their peril.

HOW TO READ THE MAPS

PRACTICALLY every map has been compiled by W. B. Alexander, who has recently retired from the Directorship of the Edward Grey Institute of Field Ornithology at Oxford.

In nearly every case the distribution has been blocked in from the *published* literature only, on a vice-county basis. Black areas represent breeding distribution ; grey areas those where the species has been observed, but not breeding ; white areas those from which the species has not been recorded. The vice-counties of Britain are shown on the following pages.

In the course of his work at the Institute, Mr. Alexander has read through all the published records of birds available in its excellent library, and nearly all others besides. Records published since approximately the beginning of this present century have been used to compile the maps published here, though Mr. Alexander has also compiled sets to show nineteenth century distribution, which are of the greatest interest to students of change.

As far as breeding distribution is concerned, there have, of course, been changes in many species since the beginning of the present century ; and the black areas have (except in special cases) been carefully arranged to represent what, on the latest information available, is considered to be the breeding distribution at the time of publication of this book. In the special cases there is some comment in the text under *Distribution* but the general object is to let the maps speak for themselves.

The black areas have not all been produced by blacking in the whole vice-counties. In the case of coastal breeding species we have simply blacked in the coastal strips concerned. In other cases the species is known to breed at definite limited stations, which can be better indicated by dots than by blacking-in.

The grey areas simply represent those vice-counties from which there has been one non-breeding record or more of the species in the twentieth century.

LIST OF VICE-COUNTIES

ENGLAND AND WALES

PENINSULA
1 West Cornwall with Scilly
2 East Cornwall
3 South Devon
4 North Devon
5 South Somerset
6 North Somerset

CHANNEL
7 North Wilts.
8 South Wilts.
9 Dorset
10 Isle of Wight
11 South Hants.
12 North Hants.
13 West Sussex
14 East Sussex

THAMES
15 East Kent
16 West Kent
17 Surrey
18 South Essex
19 North Essex
20 Hertford
21 Middlesex
22 Berks.
23 Oxford
24 Buckingham

ANGLIA
25 East Suffolk
26 West Suffolk
27 East Norfolk
28 West Norfolk
29 Cambridge
30 Bedford and detached part of Hunts.
31 Huntingdon
32 Northampton

SEVERN
33 East Gloucester
34 West Gloucester
35 Monmouth
36 Hereford
37 Worcester
38 Warwick
39 Stafford and Dudley
40 Shropshire

SOUTH WALES
41 Glamorgan
42 Brecon
43 Radnor
44 Carmarthen
45 Pembroke
46 Cardigan

NORTH WALES
47 Montgomery
48 Merioneth
49 Carnarvon
50 Denbigh and parts of Flint
51 Flint
52 Anglesey

TRENT
53 South Lincoln
54 North Lincoln
55 Leicester with Rutland
56 Nottingham
57 Derby

MERSEY
58 Cheshire
59 South Lancashire
60 Mid Lancashire

HUMBER
61 South-east York
62 North-east York
63 South-west York
64 Mid-west York
65 North-west York

TYNE
66 Durham
67 Northumberland, South
68 Cheviotland, or Northumberland, North

LAKES
69 Westmorland with North Lancashire
70 Cumberland
71 Isle of Man

SCOTLAND

W. LOWLANDS
72 Dumfries
73 Kirkcudbright
74 Wigtown
75 Ayr
76 Renfrew
77 Lanark and E. Dumbarton

E. LOWLANDS
78 Peebles
79 Selkirk
80 Roxburgh
81 Berwick
82 East Lothian
83 Midlothian
84 West Lothian

E. HIGHLANDS
85 Fife with Kinross
86 Stirling
87 South Perth with Clackmannan, and parts of Stirling
88 Mid Perth
89 North Perth
90 Angus or Forfar
91 Kincardine
92 South Aberdeen
93 North Aberdeen
94 Banff
95 Moray or Elgin
96 Easterness (East Inverness with Nairn)

W. HIGHLANDS
97 Westerness (West Inverness with North Argyll)
98 Argyll (Main)
99 Dumbarton (West)
100 Clyde Isles
101 Cantire
102 South Ebudes (Islay, etc.) and Scarba
103 Mid Ebudes (Mull, etc.)
104 North Ebudes (Skye. etc.)

N. HIGHLANDS
105 West Ross
106 East Ross
107 East Sutherland
108 West Sutherland
109 Caithness

NORTH ISLES
110 Outer Hebrides
111 Orkney
112 Shetland

IRELAND
113 South Kerry
114 North Kerry
115 West Cork
116 Mid Cork
117 East Cork
118 Waterford
119 South Tipperary
120 Limerick
121 Clare with Aran Isles
122 North Tipperary
123 Kilkenny
124 Wexford
125 Carlow
126 Leix
127 South-east Galway
128 West Galway
129 North-east Galway
130 Offaly
131 Kildare
132 Wicklow
133 Dublin
134 Meath
135 Westmeath
136 Longford
137 Roscommon
138 East Mayo
139 West Mayo
140 Sligo
141 Leitrim
142 Cavan
143 Louth
144 Monaghan
145 Fermanagh
146 East Donegal
147 West Donegal
148 Tyrone
149 Armagh
150 Down
151 Antrim
152 Derry

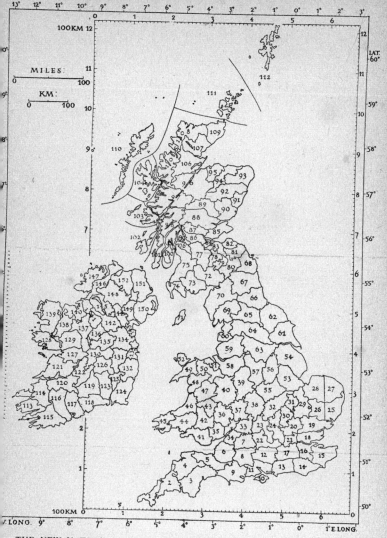

THE *NEW NATURALIST* VICE-COUNTY MAP OF THE BRITISH ISLES

Vice-Counties of the British Isles. The political divisions of Britain, *i.e.*, the simple counties, of all sorts of different shapes and sizes, and differ greatly in biological importance. The idea of the vice-county system is to divide Britain into areas of roughly equal importance, without sacrificing the county system. A glance at the map will show the sort of compromise that has been reached. Reproduced by permission of Messrs. Collins, publishers of the *New Naturalist*.

9

HOW THE YEAR-CYCLE
CHARTS WORK

THOSE woodcock which are resident in this country leave their winter haunts and feeding-grounds and begin to assemble at their breeding-grounds at the beginning of February. This assembly is usually complete at the end of March. The breeding season is a long one, the species being double-brooded. Eggs of the first brood can be found between the middle of March and the end of May; of the second brood in June and July. Young of the first brood can be found unable to fly from mid-April; and young found from the last week of June until the end of August are likely to be of the second brood.

Although all young can fly by September British resident woodcock do not normally disperse to their winter haunts until the end of October or November. By December this dispersal is complete and birds are generally in their winter quarters.

The passage of continental birds through and to Britain begins in March, a month after home birds have begun to re-assemble at their breeding haunts. The passage of continental birds is at full strength between mid-March and mid-April, and continues at diminished strength until the first week in May.

The autumn passage of continental birds begins nearly two months before the autumn dispersal of residents. Early birds pass from the last week of August to mid-September; from mid-September the main autumn passage takes place, reaching its peak at the end of October and the beginning of November. Passage continues until the end of November after which birds are generally in their winter quarters either in Britain or on the Continent.

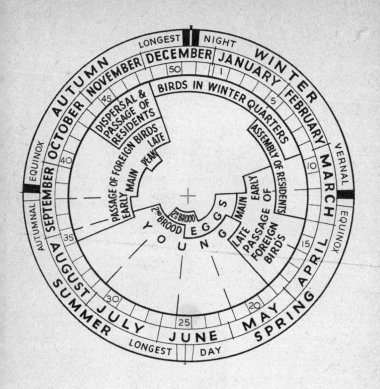

THE statement about woodcock on the opposite page took up
two-thirds of it, and described the yearly life of the woodcock in
fair detail. It is obvious that there would be no room for it in
its proper place, on page 56 or 57. The above chart, however,
gives the same information; indeed, it is more precise about
dates; and reduced in size (but not, I believe, in clarity), occupies
only a quarter of page 57.

All that is needed to read the charts is a straight edge placed
across the centre of the circle and the desired date or period.

Readers must not imagine that the periods chronicled on the
chart are accurate to within a day. The chart (like the maps)
is a first approximation to the truth and should be treated as
no more.

11

KEY: HABITAT WHEN NOT AT BREEDING-PLACE: SEA BIRDS

	OCEANS	SEAS TO EDGE OF CONTINENTAL SHELF	SEAS IN SIGHT OF ROCKY SHORES	SEAS IN SIGHT OF SANDY SHORES	ESTUARIES	INLAND WATERS	ON DRY LAND
STORM-PETREL		■	■				
LEACH'S FORK-TAILED PETREL		■	■				
GREAT SHEARWATER		■	■				
SOOTY SHEARWATER		■	■				
LITTLE AUK		■	■	■			
PUFFIN		■	■	■			
FULMAR		■	■	■			
KITTIWAKE		■	■	■			
RAZORBILL		■	■	■			
GUILLEMOT		■	■	■			
GREAT SKUA		■	■	■			
ARCTIC SKUA		■	■	■			
POMATORHINE SKUA		■	■				
LONG-TAILED SKUA		■	■				
MANX SHEARWATER		■	■	■	■		
BLACK GUILLEMOT		■	■	■	■		
GANNET		■	■	■	■		
GREAT BLACK-BACKED GULL		■	■	■	■	■	■
GLAUCOUS GULL		■	■	■	■	■	■
ICELAND GULL		■	■	■	■	■	■
COMMON GULL		■	■	■	■	■	■
HERRING-GULL		■	■	■	■	■	■
LESSER BLACK-BACKED GULL		■	■	■	■	■	■
SHAG			■	■			
ROSEATE TERN			■	■	■		
BLACK TERN			■	■	■	■	
SANDWICH TERN			■	■	■		
COMMON TERN			■	■	■	■	
ARCTIC TERN			■	■	■		
CORMORANT			■	■	■	■	
LITTLE TERN				■	■		
LITTLE GULL				■	■	■	■
BLACK-HEADED GULL				■	■	■	■
	OCEANS	SEAS TO EDGE OF CONTINENTAL SHELF	SEAS IN SIGHT OF ROCKY SHORES	SEAS IN SIGHT OF SANDY SHORES	ESTUARIES	INLAND WATERS	ON DRY LAND

KEY: HABITAT WHEN NOT AT BREEDING-PLACE: WADERS

	AT SEA	ROCKY SHORES	ESTUARIES, OPEN SANDS AND FLATS	ESTUARINE CREEKS, SALT MARSH GUTTERS	RIVERS, STREAMS AND THEIR BANKS	LAKES RESERVOIRS AND THEIR BORDERS	MARSHES, BOGGY POOLS AND SEWAGE FARMS	DRY OPEN LAND	WOOD-LAND
GREY PHALAROPE	■								
RED-NECKED PHALAROPE	■								
REDSHANK			■	■	■		■		
SPOTTED REDSHANK			■	■		■	■		
COMMON SANDPIPER				■	■	■	■		
PURPLE SANDPIPER		■	■						
TURNSTONE		■	■	■					
OYSTERCATCHER		■	■	■		■	■		
WHIMBREL		■	■	■			■	■	
CURLEW		■	■	■		■	■	■	
DOTTEREL								■	
GOLDEN PLOVER			■	■			■	■	
LAPWING					■	■	■	■	
RINGED PLOVER			■	■		■	■		
LITTLE RINGED PLOVER					■	■			
KENTISH PLOVER			■	■					
AVOCET			■	■					
DUNLIN			■	■		■	■		
CURLEW-SANDPIPER			■	■			■		
BLACK-TAILED GODWIT			■	■			■		
BAR-TAILED GODWIT		■	■	■					
KNOT			■	■					
SANDERLING		■	■	■					
GREY PLOVER		■	■	■					
LITTLE STINT			■	■		■	■		
TEMMINCK'S STINT				■		■	■		
GREEN SANDPIPER				■	■	■	■		
GREENSHANK				■	■	■	■		
BLACK-WINGED STILT						■	■		
SNIPE					■	■	■		
JACK SNIPE							■		
CRANE							■	■	
RUFF						■	■	■	
WOOD-SANDPIPER						■	■		
WOODCOCK							■	■	■
STONE-CURLEW								■	■
GREAT BUSTARD								■	
LITTLE BUSTARD								■	
	AT SEA	ROCKY SHORES	ESTUARIES, OPEN SANDS AND FLATS	ESTUARINE CREEKS, SALT MARSH GUTTERS	RIVERS, STREAMS AND THEIR BANKS	LAKES RESERVOIRS AND THEIR BORDERS	MARSHES, BOGGY POOLS AND SEWAGE FARMS	DRY OPEN LAND	WOOD-LAND

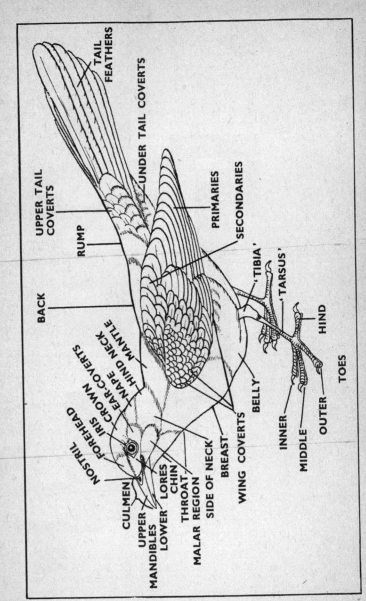

TAIL FEATHERS

UPPER TAIL COVERTS

UNDER TAIL COVERTS

RUMP

BACK

PRIMARIES

SECONDARIES

'TIBIA'

'TARSUS'

HIND

TOES

MANTLE

HIND NECK

NAPE

EAR-COVERTS

IRIS

CROWN

FOREHEAD

NOSTRIL

CULMEN

UPPER

LOWER MANDIBLES

LORES

CHIN

THROAT

MALAR REGION

SIDE OF NECK

BREAST

WING COVERTS

BELLY

INNER

MIDDLE

OUTER

HOW TO USE THE FIELD CHARACTER KEYS

No key is perfect. Every system that has been devised for running down something by a process of elimination has this common fault ; that once the user has taken the wrong turning it is difficult for him to get back on the rails again. It is my hope that users of the sea-bird and wader identification keys that follow will be able to keep on the rails. I have tried to avoid, as much as possible, suggesting size as a key to the distinction between any two species or groups. But sometimes size *must* be used. Lest my use of the words " small," " medium-large," " immense," etc., etc. be thought vague I must state at once that they have exact meanings, corresponding to the length of the bird in its normal live posture, excluding the bill in the long-billed species. The meanings are as follows :—

Adjective	Length in inches	Adjective	Length in inches
Minute	4-6	Medium-large ..	20-24
Very small ..	6-8	Large	24-28
Small	8-12	Very large ..	28-32
Small-medium ..	12-16	Immense ..	32-36
Medium	16-20	Gigantic	over 36

There are no tiny birds (length under 4 inches) mentioned in this volume.

To show the key in action, let us take an example from the wader key. You are walking, one day late in July, along the broad white beach of the island of Tiree in the Inner Hebrides. A flock of small birds with grey backs settles and proceeds to scuttle along the sands in a very busy way, packed close. The flock takes wing and pitches again in a few yards, during which you have time to note : rumps not white, but some white on tail. Some of the birds are very whitish about head and underparts ; others have a certain amount of chestnut-brown on head and neck, or so it appears. You cannot get bill and leg colour exactly but they look dark, and birds have general build of dunlins (which you have seen before) but look very fat. They are clearly waders. The birds are not bustards or cranes ; so, in the wader key, 1(c) takes us to 2. Our birds are not medium-sized (they are nowhere near 16 inches long) ; nor are their bills shorter than their heads ; so 2(b) takes us to 4 and, as the birds are not conspicuously pied, 4(b) to 6(b) to 13. Their bills are not *much* longer than their heads, so 13(*b*) to 22. The birds have *some* white in their tails ; and anyway are not the least like snipe in plumage or habit ; so 22(*b*) takes us to 23.

Under 23 we decide that the choice is between (*a*) and (*c*). The birds are certainly not turnstones (*b*). We decide that the answer is (*c*) as the birds are not delicate in build and show no signs of swimming. But we make a mental reservation to try again *via* (*a*) if we come into a blind alley *via* (*c*). 23(*c*) takes us to 25 ; and as the birds' rumps are not white or pale 25(*a*) takes us to 26. In 26 the choice is clear ; though we have forgotten to look for a wing-bar we see that our birds satisfy " plump," " runs swiftly " and " sands," all of which apply to 26(*a*) and not 26(*b*). Our waders are certainly not minute (26(*c*)). 26(*a*) takes us to 27. In 27 we can see that, of the three birds to choose from, SANDERLING fits our birds exactly ; it fits both those with white and those with chestnut. Purple sandpiper is no fit at all. Dunlin is out as if in winter plumage it would have a dark head, and if in summer plumage black on the lower breast.

We can conclude, then, that we have a flock of sanderlings, some of which still wear part if not all of their breeding dress. Looking up page 81 we see that the autumn migration of sanderlings down the west coast of Britain contains elements which are likely to pass through Tiree ; and (from the year-cycle chart) that the birds we see, moving in late July, constitute *early* autumn passengers ; are, in fact, in advance of the main stream.

FIELD CHARACTER KEY TO BRITISH SEA-BIRDS

1 *a* Birds with small, narrow wings which fly with very rapid wing-beats, and which do not glide or soar .. AUKS ; *see* 2
  b Birds with large wings which fly with relatively slow wing-beats, and which glide and soar .. .. .. *see* 6
2 AUKS. Small to medium ; plumage black or dark brown and white. Upright carriage on land.
  a Medium .. .. *see* 3
  b Small or small-medium .. .. *see* 4
3 *a* Deep, laterally compressed black bill crossed by nearly vertical white line ; black upper-parts, white under-parts ; black legs and feet .. .. RAZORBILL (p. 162)
  b Slender pointed black bill ; dark brown upper-parts, white under-parts ; in winter dark streak behind eye ; yellowish legs and feet .. .. .. GUILLEMOT (p. 166)

4 *a* Small; dumpy bird with very short black bill; black
   upper-parts, white under-parts; legs and feet brown-
   black   ..   ..   LITTLE AUK (p. 170)
   b Small-medium ..   .. *see* 5

5 *a* Triangular, parrot-like bill (blue, yellow and red in summer,
   brown and orange in winter); black upper-parts, white
   under-parts; legs and feet red in summer, yellow in
   winter   ..   ..   PUFFIN (p. 172)
   b Pointed black bill; black except for large white patch on
   wing in summer; mainly white in winter with pronounced
   blackish mottling on back and neck; legs and feet red
   BLACK GUILLEMOT (p. 168)

6 *a* GANNET: very large; body in flight cigar-shaped; plunges
   when fishing from height of up to 140 ft., nearly always
   stays under for at least 5 seconds; 6 ft. wing-spread, black
   ends to wings; rest of plumage in adults white with yellow
   on head, in young blackish speckled with white, black
   gradually lost in 4 years of youth; powerful bluish-white
   bill; legs black-brown with green lines GANNET (p. 34)
   b Very small to large; if plunge from air when fishing never
   do so from very great height, and stay under for only a
   second ..   .. *see* 7

7 *a* Long-necked birds; upright carriage on land
   CORMORANT and SHAG; *see* 8
   b Short-necked birds; horizontal carriage on land; small
   to large ..   .. *see* 9

8 **CORMORANT and SHAG.** Medium-large or large ; dark
   plumage ; long brownish bills hooked at tip ; legs and
   feet dark ; dive from surface, under about a minute.
   a Large ; adult has black and bronze plumage with white
   sides of face and chin ; in summer white patch on thigh ;
   no crest, grey-white plumes on head ; young has brown
   upper-parts, under-parts whitish mottled with brown
   CORMORANT (p. 31)
   b Medium-large ; slim ; adult with dark green plumage
   with no white ; in summer distinct crest ; young have
   upper- and under-parts brown . . . SHAG (p. 32)

9 *a* Very small or small sooty birds with white rumps
   STORM and LEACH'S PETRELS ; *see* 10
   b Small to large birds ; if dark have not white rumps *see* 11

10 **STORM and LEACH'S PETRELS.** Tubular nostrils ; bill, legs and feet black.

   a Very small ; square-tailed ; fluttering bat-like flight ; habitually follows vessels . STORM-PETREL (p. 36)

   b Small ; fork-tailed ; darting and gliding buoyant flight, does not follow vessels

         LEACH'S FORK-TAILED PETREL (p. 38)

11 *a* Small-medium to medium birds with long narrow wings, which are held very straight out in flight ; fly in long, tilted glides on stiffly extended wings with intervals of a few wing-beats ; tubular nostrils

         SHEARWATERS and FULMAR ; *see* 12

   b Small to large birds with broader wings which in flight are somewhat angled about half-way along leading edge ; normal flight steady flapping and when glide tend to adopt horizontal rather than tilted posture ; nostrils normal

         GULLS, SKUAS and TERNS ; *see* 15

12 **FULMAR and SHEARWATERS.**

   a Medium ; grey above, yellow-white under-parts ; or entirely grey ; fairly short, heavy bill ; does not swim under water ; no black tips to wings ; bill-colour variable ; legs and feet bluish . . . . FULMAR (p. 45)

   b Small-medium or medium ; black or sooty above, white or sooty under-parts ; elongated slender bill somewhat hooked at tip ; can swim under water

         SHEARWATERS ; *see* 13

13 *a* Medium ; entirely sooty-black except for pale line under wing ; bill, legs and feet blackish

         SOOTY SHEARWATER (p. 43)

   b Small-medium or medium ; dark above and white under-parts . . . . *see* 14

14 *a* Small-medium ; black above, white under-parts ; bill dark, legs and feet pink and black ; does not follow boats

         MANX SHEARWATER (p. 40)

   b Medium ; dark brown above, white under-parts—more white than *a*—on neck white nearly meets across nape, bird thus appears to have brown cap ; white patch also at base of tail (not amounting to white rump) ; bill dark, legs and feet whitish and brown ; follows fishing-boats

         GREAT SHEARWATER (p. 42)

15 *a* Small-medium to medium-large ; plumage uniformly dark brown ; mostly dark brown ; dark brown on crown, back and wings ; or *barred* with grey or brown ; bill black or brown, legs and feet black or grey and black ; carnivorous and piratical habits—make other birds disgorge food

SKUAS ; *see* 16

   b Small to large ; plumage slate-grey ; grey-black and white ; grey and white ; almost white ; or *mottled* with grey or brown ; bill and legs never *both* black ; piratical habits rare . . TERNS and GULLS ; *see* 19

16 SKUAS.

   a Medium-large ; uniform brown with white patch in middle of leading edge of wing ; central tail feathers not elongated ; bill, legs and feet dull black

GREAT SKUA (p. 154)

   b Small-medium or medium, two phases. *Dark :* uniform brown (if so no white patch on wing) ; or *Light :* in summer brown with yellowish sides of neck ; whitish nape, throat and under-parts ; in winter barred brown and whitish . . . . *see* 17

   c Small-medium or medium ; nearly uniform brown ; or head, neck and back barred brown and buff, under-parts barred blackish, brown and whitish ; *almost impossible to distinguish from each other in the field*

YOUNG POMATORHINE, ARCTIC and LONG-TAILED SKUAS (pp. 156-61)

17 *a* Small-medium ; two very long, slender, middle tail-feathers, up to 8 in. long ; bill black, legs grey, feet black ; Dark phase extremely rare

LONG-TAILED SKUA (p. 160)

   b Medium ; two middle tail-feathers project up to 3 in. ; bill brown, legs black ; dark phase not rare . . *see* 18

18 *a* Medium ; larger and more robust than *b* ; central tail-feathers broad, blunt and *twisted* ; dark phase 1 in 7 among British migrants POMATORHINE SKUA (p. 156)

   b Medium ; central tail-feathers narrow, pointed, not twisted ; dark phase 5 in 6 among British breeders

ARCTIC SKUA (p. 158)

19 *a* Small to medium ; nearly uniform slate-grey ; or white and grey with black caps ; light and buoyant deliberate flight, rising and sinking at each wing-beat

TERNS ; *see* 20

19 *b* Small to large ; whitish ; grey and white, or grey-black and white ; sometimes whole head black or dark brown ; steady, soaring flight . . . . **GULLS** ; *see* 26

20 **TERNS.** Slender, graceful birds with tapering bills and forked tails.

   a Small ; uniform slate-grey and black except for white under tail ; bill black ; legs and feet red-brown
   BLACK TERN (SUMMER) (p. 124)

   b Small to medium ; black cap, grey back and wings, white under-parts . . . . *see* 21

21 *a* Small . . . . *see* 22
   b Small-medium and medium . . . . *see* 23

22 *a* Black cap, white forehead, under-parts white ; back and wings grey ; grey extends down as patch on under-parts in front of base of wing ; bill black, legs and feet red-brown . . . **BLACK TERN (WINTER)** (p. 124)

   b Black cap, white forehead in *summer* and winter ; back and wings grey, no patch on white under-parts ; bill, legs and feet yellow . . . **LITTLE TERN** (p. 134)

23 *a* Medium ; tail slightly forked ; wings very long and narrow ; bill black with yellow tip ; legs and feet black, with yellow soles, comparatively long ; flight more gull-like than *b* . . . **SANDWICH TERN** (p. 126)

   b Small-medium ; tail markedly forked ; wings not as long as *a* ; bill red and black ; legs and feet red to orange *see* 24

24 *a* Whiter appearance than *b* ; bill black, with red at base in summer ; very long tail-streamers ; alarm-note hoarse " ach, ach " . . . **ROSEATE TERN** (p. 128)

   b Greyer than *a* ; bill red, or nearly all red in summer, black, or nearly all black, in winter ; tail-streamers do not normally extend beyond tips of folded wings ; alarm-note harsh " kee-ar " . . . . *see* 25

25 *a* Black tip to red bill in summer ; in winter bill black with some red remaining at base ; relatively long legs ; in alarm-note accent on first syllable of " kee-ar "
   COMMON TERN (p. 130)

   b Pure red bill in summer changing by stages to pure black bill in winter ; relatively short legs ; in alarm-note accent on second syllable of " kee-ar "
   ARCTIC TERN (p. 132)

   It is extremely difficult *to tell juvenile or winter common and arctic terns apart and mistakes are to be expected.*

26 GULLS.
  a Small to medium . . . . *see* 27
  b Medium-large or large . . . . . *see* 39

27 *a* Head wholly dark . . . . . . *see* 28
  b Head wholly or partly white . . . . *see* 29

28 *a* Small ; head black ; no black on wings but dark slaty
    undersides ; bill red-brown, legs vermilion
                LITTLE GULL (SUMMER) (p. 136)
  b Small-medium ; head brown ; black tips and white front
    margin to wings ; bill and legs crimson
        BLACK-HEADED GULL (SUMMER) (p. 138)

29 *a* Tail with black band at or near end . . . *see* 30
  b Tail white . . . . *see* 33

30 *a* Under-side of wing and body spotted and mottled brown ;
    medium ; head grey-brown streaked white, back brown,
    upper-side wings brown and grey with black-brown ends,
    no white at tips ; bill blackish, legs yellow-flesh
        YOUNG COMMON GULL (p. 140, *see also* 38)
  b Under-side of wing and body white, or white and grey
                        see 31

31 *a* Black diagonal bar across upper-side of wings . *see* 32
  b Broad white margin to front edge of wings, which have
    black tips and dark mottling ; small-medium ; crown
    mottled brown ; bill dull flesh, legs yellowish flesh ; grey
    back . YOUNG BLACK-HEADED GULL (p. 138)

32 *a* Small ; dark crown ; bill blackish, legs dull red-brown or
    flesh ; back sooty barred with white
                YOUNG LITTLE GULL (p. 136)
  b Medium ; head white with blackish ear-patch, back of
    head grey ; bill green, legs brown ; back spotted blackish
    with broad black band on back of neck
               YOUNG KITTIWAKE (p. 152)

33 *a* Small ; under-side wing dark slaty ; bill blackish ; no
    black on upper-side of wing
               LITTLE GULL (WINTER) (p. 136)
  b Small-medium or medium ; under-side wing white and
    grey ; bill from red to yellow-green ; black ends to upper-
    side of wing . . . . *see* 34

34 *a* Small-medium ; crimson bill and legs ; broad white margin to front of wing

   BLACK-HEADED GULL (WINTER) (p. 138)

   b Medium ; bill and legs not red ; no white margin to front of wing . . . . *see* 35

35 *a* Wings with pure black ends ; bill yellow, legs brown-black . . . . *see* 36

   b Wings with black ends tipped with white ; bill and legs yellow-green . . . . *see* 37

36 *a* Head white . . KITTIWAKE (SUMMER) (p. 152)
   b Head greyish . KITTIWAKE (WINTER) (p. 152)

37 *a* Head white . COMMON GULL (SUMMER) (p. 140)
   b Head strongly streaked dusky brown

   COMMON GULL (WINTER) (p. 140)

38 The medium COMMON GULL is also likely to be confused with the medium-large HERRING-GULL. The herring-gull is *very definitely larger*, has a slower wing-beat, and a thicker and more powerful bill. Its wings, at rest, do not project so far beyond its tail. Its legs at all ages are flesh-coloured and are less yellow than those of the immature and less green than those of the adult common gull. The adult herring-gull's bill is yellow with a red spot ; the adult common gull's is yellow-green with no red spot. The common gull's *eye*, in the field, appears to be much larger and darker than that of the herring-gull.

39 *a* Bill yellow with red spot ; head white, streaked with brown in winter ; tail and under-parts white . . . *see* 40

   b Bill black, or black and yellow ; plumage various shades of brown, mottled . . . . *see* 45

40 *a* Mantle and wings dark slate-grey to black . . *see* 41
   b Mantle and wings grey . . . . . *see* 43

41 *a* Medium-large, legs yellow ; bill less massive . *see* 42
   b Large ; legs whitish-flesh ; bill massive ; mantle and wings black GREAT BLACK-BACKED GULL (p. 146)

42 *a* Mantle and wings dark slate grey

   BRITISH LESSER BLACK-BACKED GULL (p. 144)

   b Mantle and wings black

   SCANDINAVIAN LESSER BLACK-BACKED GULL (p. 144)

43 *a* Mantle and wings grey ; wings with black ends on which
white spots (*see also* 38) . HERRING-GULL (p. 142)
  b Mantle and wings light grey ; no black on wings . *see* 44

44 *a* Large ; ring round eye lemon yellow ; tips of wings
folded to tip of tail ; bill massive
GLAUCOUS GULL (p. 148)
  b Medium-large ; ring round eye brick-red ; tips of wings
folded beyond tip of tail ; bill less massive
ICELAND GULL (p. 150)

45 *a* Mottling coarse ; ends of wings sooty-brown to black,
dark band near tip of tail . . . . . . *see* 46
  b Mottling fine and uniform, including ends of wings and
tail . . . . *see* 48

46 *a* Large ; head, tail and under-parts whiter ; pattern of
mottling more contrasted ; bill more massive than *b*
YOUNG GREAT BLACK-BACKED GULL (p. 146)
  b Medium-large ; head, tail and under-parts brown ; bill
less massive . . . . *see* 47

47 Until they are about a year old, it is extremely difficult, if
not impossible, to distinguish in the field, YOUNG
HERRING- and LESSER BLACK-BACKED GULLS,
though in the later stages of immature plumage, when the
mantle and wing-colour of the adult begins to appear,
distinction is easier.   On the whole, young immature lesser
black-backed gulls tend to be darker, with browner tails.

48 *a* Large ; tips of wings folded to tip of tail ; bill massive
YOUNG GLAUCOUS GULL (p. 148)
  b Medium-large ; tips of wings folded beyond tip of tail ;
bill less massive . YOUNG ICELAND GULL (p. 150)

FIELD CHARACTER KEY TO BRITISH WADERS

1 *a* Immense ; sandy upper-parts barred with black ; heavy
body ; much white in wing in flight
GREAT BUSTARD (p. 118)

 b Very large ; uniformly grey body ; long neck ; relatively
short beak ; long legs ; secondary feathers of wing form
what looks like festooned tail when bird at rest ; red patch
on back of head.   Distinguishable at once from herons and
stork by relative length of bill and loud clanging notes in
flight .   .   .   . CRANE (p. 122)

 c Minute to medium .   .   .   .   .   . *see* 2

2 *a* Medium birds with bills shorter than head .   . *see* 3

 b Minute to small-medium birds ; and medium birds with
bills longer than head .   .   .   .   .   . *see* 4

3 *a* Sandy mantle and white under-parts ; males in summer
pattern of bluish, white and black on head and neck ; much
white on wing and general white appearance in flight
LITTLE BUSTARD (p. 120)

 b Sandy plumage generally ; large yellow eye ; white and
black pattern on wing in flight ; call " coo-ee "
STONE-CURLEW (p. 116)

4 *a* Medium or small-medium birds, conspicuously pied *see* 5

 b Minute to small birds ; and medium and small-medium
birds not conspicuously pied .   .   .   .   . *see* 6

5 *a* Medium ; upper-parts glossy black except white wing-bar
and rump ; under-parts white ; long orange bill ; pink
legs ; noisy shrill piping OYSTERCATCHER (p. 114)

 b Small-medium ; white plumage with bold black bands on
crown and back of neck, back and wings ; long, upcurved
black bill ; very long blue-grey legs . AVOCET (p. 112)

 c Small-medium ; white plumage with black mantle and
wings ; summer male has black on head ; long straight
black bill ; immensely long pink legs
BLACK-WINGED STILT (p. 110)

 d Small-medium ; upper-parts metallic green with white
rump and white on head ; under-parts white with black
on breast and reddish under tail ; conspicuous crest ;
short black bill ; brown legs ; in flight rounded wings ;
call " pee-wit " .   .   .   . LAPWING (p. 108)

6 *a* Bill swollen towards tip, and not as long as head . *see* 7

  b Bill tapering towards tip, and as long as, or longer than head . . . . *see* 13

7 *a* Small ; no white collar . . . . . . *see* 8

  b Very small and robust ; conspicuous white collar and under-parts . . . . *see* 11

8 *a* Smaller than *b* ; broad white eye-stripes meeting at back of head ; dark breast separated from chestnut belly by white band ; legs dull yellow ; piping note " wit-e-wee "
                       DOTTEREL (p. 106)

  b Larger than *a* ; upper-parts spangled dark and light ; under-parts light in winter, mostly dark in summer ; legs grey . . . . *see* 9

9 *a* Upper-parts spangled black and gold ; slender bill ; patch of white feathers in axilla under wing ; dark rump and tail ; no wing-bar . . . . *see* 10

  b Upper-parts spangled black and grey (some yellow on young) ; stouter bill ; in winter upper-parts less spangled, more uniform than *a* ; patch of black feathers in axilla under wing ; whitish rump, tail and wing-bar
                      GREY PLOVER (p. 104)

10 *a* Under-parts whitish with some dark mottlings ; impossible to distinguish subspecies in field
          GOLDEN PLOVER (WINTER) (p. 102)

  b Face, cheeks and under-parts black separated by broad white band from upper-parts
  NORTHERN GOLDEN PLOVER (SUMMER) (p. 102)

  c Face dusky, throat mottled, black on breast and belly only, and flecked with light feathers ; no pure white band
  SOUTHERN GOLDEN PLOVER (SUMMER) (p. 102)

11 *a* Legs yellow-flesh ; black band round breast ; wide dark band " through " eye . . . . . . *see* 12

  b Legs lead-grey ; dark patches on sides of breast ; narrow dark band " through " eye ; bill black
             KENTISH PLOVER (p. 100)

12 *a* Larger than *b* ; white wing-bar ; note liquid " tooi " ; legs usually bright yellow . RINGED PLOVER (p. 96)

  b Smaller than *a* ; no wing-bar ; note higher-pitched " teu " ; legs dull flesh
        LITTLE RINGED PLOVER (p. 98)

13 *a* Bills considerably longer than head . . . *see* 14

  b Minute to small birds with bills not very much longer than head . . . . *see* 22

14 *a* Long bills curved downwards . . . . . *see* 15
   b Straight or upcurved bills . . . . . . *see* 16

15 *a* Medium ; very long, strongly downcurved bill ; streaky-brown plumage with no distinctive pattern on crown ; usual cry " croo-ee " . . . . CURLEW (p. 52)
   b Small-medium ; relatively shorter downcurved bill ; streaky brown plumage with two dark bands on crown divided by pale streak ; usual cry a trilling titter
                       WHIMBREL (p. 54)

16 *a* Bill straight or upcurved ; white rumps or tails . *see* 17
   b Bill straight ; plumage dark (no white rump or tail) with rich pattern of stripes . . . . *see* 21

17 *a* Very long bill ; plumage curlew-like but males assume chestnut colour in summer ; legs dark ; whickering note . . . . *see* 18
   b Long bill ; usually grey-brown plumage ; legs red or green ; note a piping whistle . . . *see* 19

18 *a* Small-medium ; bill noticeably upcurved ; feet only project slightly beyond tail in flight ; *no wing-bar* ; rump dull white, tail barred (looks dirty white) ; underparts whiter than curlew, breast only faintly streaked ; male assumes rufous plumage in breeding-season
               BAR-TAILED GODWIT (p. 48)
   b Medium ; bill only faintly upcurved, longer than *a* ; legs project beyond tail in flight, longer than *a* ; *broad white wing-bar* ; rump dark but tail pure white with broad black band near tip ; under-parts in winter light grey rather than white and back brown-grey, darker and more uniform than *a* ; in breeding-season rufous plumage mostly restricted to breast, belly and under-tail remaining whitish
              BLACK-TAILED GODWIT (p. 50)

19 *a* Small or small-medium ; red or orange-yellow legs ; red or orange straight bill ; white spots or white margin on wing . . . . *see* 20
   b Small-medium ; greenish legs ; blue-slate slightly up-curved bill ; *no white on wing* ; feet project beyond tail in flight ; note " too-too-too," lower than redshank
                 GREENSHANK (p. 94)

20 *a* Small ; legs orange-red (yellow in young) ; *broad white crescent on hind border of wing* ; upper-parts brown and grey winter, marked with black summer ; feet only project slightly beyond tail in flight ; note " too," and " too-oo-oo," higher than greenshank . REDSHANK (p. 90)

  b Small-medium ; legs very dark red ; *white spots but no marginal crescent on wing* ; plumage (upper and under) very dark, spotted or streaked with white in summer (rump of course white as in all " shanks " described here), in winter more ashy grey than redshank on upper-parts, white under-parts ; feet and part of legs project beyond tail in flight ; note " chew-it "

                        SPOTTED REDSHANK (p. 92)

21 *a* Small-medium ; very long straight bill ; stout build ; rich plumage pattern gives " marbled " impression ; rises without voice but often clap of wings ; wings appear rounded in flight ; a woodland species . WOODCOCK (p. 56)

  b Small ; long straight bill ; finer build than *a* ; plumage pattern gives " barred " impression ; pale central stripe on crown ; rises with hoarse note and zig-zag flight ; wings appear pointed in flight ; a marsh and meadow species

                                     SNIPE (p. 58)

22 *a* Very small snipe-like bird with dark plumage (no white on tail) and rich pattern of stripes giving " mottled " impression ; bill relatively shorter than that of snipe ; two pale stripes over eye separated by narrow black stripe ; rises reluctantly, usually silently and with slower and straighter flight than snipe ; marshes and bogs

                            JACK SNIPE (p. 60)

  b Minute to small waders, not snipe-like, with white rumps or tails, or at least some white on rump or tail . *see* 23

23 *a* Tail much rounded ; habitually swim, lobed feet ; females in summer brighter than males ; buoyant and delicate

                                    see 24

  b Tail slightly rounded ; small birds with conical short pointed black bill, rather thick at base, slightly upcurved ; at rest upper-parts have mottled " tortoiseshell " appearance ; broad dark band on breast ; bold pied pattern in flight ; legs orange . . . TURNSTONE (p. 66)

  c Tail square or graduated, not rounded ; do not normally swim ; feet not lobed ; less delicate ; bill dark ; not pied . . . . *see* 25

24 *a* Small ; yellow base of bill, shorter and broader than *b* ; all under-parts chestnut ; sides of face whitish ; back striped brown, buff, chestnut
GREY PHALAROPE (SUMMER) (p. 62)

  b Very small ; black bill, longer and finer than *a* ; under-parts and throat white ; orange band on sides of neck and upper breast ; back slate grey
RED-NECKED PHALAROPE (SUMMER) (p. 64)

  c Small ; bill shorter and broader than *d* ; back grey, more uniform than *d* ; under-parts white
GREY PHALAROPE (WINTER) (p. 62)

  d Very small ; bill longer and finer than *c* ; back darker grey with whitish streaks, less uniform than *c* ; wings darker than *c* and white wing-bar more prominent ; under-parts white
RED-NECKED PHALAROPE (WINTER) (p. 64)

25 *a* Rump-tail area dark in centre with white at sides . *see* 26
  b Rump-tail area white or pale giving appearance of light patch in flight . . . . *see* 30

26 *a* Very small or small ; plump or round-shouldered appearance ; runs swiftly ; usually found outside breeding-season on rocky shores, sands or open flats ; flocks can perform aerial evolutions ; distinct white wing-bar . *see* 27
  b Very small or small ; more slender appearance ; outside breeding-season in coastal areas, creeks and rocky inlets, otherwise inland ; flocks rare and do not perform aerial evolutions . . . . *see* 28
  c Minute, the smallest British waders ; narrow white wing-bar not very conspicuous . . . . . *see* 29

27 *a* Small ; slightly larger than *b* ; plump ; black bill and legs ; very active runner ; white wing-bar more prominent than in *b* ; in winter adult has upper-parts pale grey with faint dark markings, most of head and all under-parts white (phalaropes, *see* 24, which in winter might be confused, have dark patch on face and are slender, not plump), and dark front to wing ; in summer quite different from *b* ; with whole head, neck, breast light chestnut and same on back mottled with black ; note " twick-twick " ; beaches and open flats . . . . SANDERLING (p. 80)
  b Very small, but only slightly smaller than *a* ; typical " round-shouldered " appearance ; black bill fairly long, may be straight or slightly downcurved, legs dark olive ;

active runner but not as fast as *a* ; white wing-bar definite but less prominent than in *a* ; in winter much less white than *a* ; brownish-grey with throat, belly and under-tail alone white ; in summer mantle becomes chestnut and black, and black patch on lower breast ; note " twerp," beaches and open flats . . . DUNLIN (p. 70)

c Small ; larger than *b* ; robust and portly ; bill brown-black, yellow at base, legs dull yellow ; active runner ; white wing-bar noticeable in flight ; winter plumage noticeably dark ; back dark blackish ; head, neck and breast sooty brown ; throat and belly white ; rufous edging to feathers in summer ; note " wheat-wit " but often rises silent ; *rocky* coastal areas

PURPLE SANDPIPER (p. 78)

28 *a* Very small ; slender ; typical bobbing motion of body ; very typical low flicking flight with short glides, wings appear curiously bent, well-defined wing-bar ; upper-parts brownish grey flecked with dark in summer ; breast streaked ashy, rest of under-parts white ; shrill note " twee-wee-wee " ; estuaries but mostly inland by rocky shores and streams . COMMON SANDPIPER (p. 84)

b Small ; heavier than *a* ; erect stance ; rapid strong flight ; narrow, not very clear, white wing-bar ; light areas on each side of dark central area of tail give impression of clear oval white patches ; young on autumn passage most often seen ; back has bold black-brown pattern, rich buff breast, throat and rest of under-parts white. Summer female similar but greyer and tendency towards barring on breast. Sexes alike in winter (except males (ruffs) larger than females (reeves)) when colour tends towards fairly uniform grey. In summer males assume the ruffs and ear-tufts, of a great variety of colour-schemes, which make identification a matter of no difficulty. Usually silent, but note " tu-whit " ; estuaries but mostly inland by marshy shores and bogs . . . . . . RUFF (p. 82)

29 *a* In summer upper-parts mainly rufous and buff mottled black, in winter ashy-brown ; under-parts mostly white ; voice " chit, chit, chit " ; habits rather like dunlin, frequents sands and flats in flocks which perform evolutions

LITTLE STINT (p. 74)

29 *b* In summer darker, duller and less rufous than *a* and in winter greyer ; under-parts white but definite grey breast ; voice a trilling titter ; mainly inland and fresh-water species ; breeds among open scrubland near water ; flocks smaller than those of *a* and do not perform evolutions

TEMMINCK'S STINT (p. 76)

30 *a* Small or very small ; grey and white in winter ; rich chestnut in summer ; " dunlin-like " ; haunt sands and flats in flocks . . . . *see* 31

   b Small ; dark and white in winter and summer ; " sand-piper-like " ; haunt mainly inland marshes but also creeks . . . . *see* 32

31 *a* Small ; bill straight and rather short ; legs rather short ; not very conspicuous white wing-bar ; white lower rump and tail with black barring appears as pale patch ; a stocky bird, the largest shore wader of the dunlin type, haunts open flats in great flocks ; voice " knot " KNOT (p. 68)

   b Compare carefully with dunlin (27*b*) from which main difference is white rump. Very small ; bill downcurved, longish and fine ; legs longer than dunlin ; fairly conspicuous white wing-bar ; clear white rump ; in winter contrast of grey and white " cleaner " than in dunlin ; often flocks with dunlin ; voice " chirrup "

CURLEW-SANDPIPER (p. 72)

32 *a* Larger, stouter and darker ; legs shorter than *b* ; under-side of wing blackish ; upper-parts appear black in winter, under-parts white, grey on breast ; in summer white spotting on dark mantle finer than *b* and breast less streaked ; white patch extends from rump over most of tail ; voice " tweet-weet-weet "

GREEN SANDPIPER (p. 88)

   b Smaller, more slender, lighter ; legs longer than *a* ; under-sider of wing light grey ; upper-parts appear mottled grey-brown in winter, under-parts more heavily marked than in *a* with head, neck and breast streaked grey-brown ; in summer back conspicuously mottled and chequered with white markings and breast horizontally streaked ; white patch less bold than *a* (but still conspicuous) as confined to rump, tail barred ; voice " chiff-chiff "

WOOD-SANDPIPER (p. 86)

CORMORANT *Phalacrocorax carbo* (LINNAEUS) 1758.

CORMORANT (upper) and SHAG, summer plumage, about 1/16

RECOGNITION. Large. Length about 3 ft., wing-spread 4½ft. Long brownish bill hooked at tip. Legs and feet dark. Adult has black and bronze plumage with white sides to face and chin and in summer white patch on side of thigh. No crest; grey-white plumes on head. Young have brown upper-parts; under-parts whitish mottled with brown. Normally flies low over water, but inland birds may fly high, occasionally mounting in spirals until out of sight, which may be at distance of 3,000 ft. Dives from surface of water, swims with legs not wings, and usually stays under half a minute. Feeds on fish, flat and round equally. Voice a hoarse " korr " with variations, mainly at breeding-place.

BREEDING. Social. Display mutual ; birds raise tail and throw head right back over back. Male slowly flaps wings. Nests, when crowded, each occupy about 4 sq. ft. : built mainly of seaweed, or sticks and grass inland. May be on low rocks, on broad cliff-ledges, or even in trees. 3-6 eggs, normally 4, length 2½ in., chalky white deposit on blue. Both sexes incubate 4 weeks ; both feed young for 5 weeks or more : nestling blackish, soon covered dark brown down. Young probably does not breed until fourth season after that in which it is hatched.

DISTRIBUTION. British resident race is *Phalacrocorax c. carbo*, also found from White Sea to Norway, Iceland, Greenland and Gulf of St. Lawrence. Southern race, *P. c. sinensis*, occurs S.E. and S. coasts England autumn and winter, otherwise in Europe S. of Baltic, Asia and N. Africa : cannot in winter be recognised as different from *P. c. carbo* : in summer much white on head. Almost the only southern birds recognised in Britain have been " ringed " on continent. Cormorants feed within sight of shore, in seas and estuaries : also in rivers and fresh-water lakes.

MOVEMENTS. Significant S.W. autumn movement of birds, mostly young ; most adults stay near breeding-place.

TO READ. D. Gunn (1927). *On a soaring cormorant.* British Birds, vol. 21, pp. 82-5.

SHAG *Phalacrocorax aristotelis* (LINNAEUS) 1761.

RECOGNITION. Medium-large. Length about 2½ ft., wing-spread 3½ ft. Bill, legs and feet dark. Slim. Adult has dark green plumage with no white. Distinct up-curved crest in summer. Young have upper- and under-parts brown, without white. Sometimes swims under water with wings as well as legs, and usually stays under nearly a minute. Feeds on fish, more round than flat fish. Voice a hoarse croak, at breeding-place.

BREEDING. Social or solitary. Display much as cormorant's; initiative with female. Nests seldom crowded, and mostly individually placed on small ledges or " brackets " on cliffs, often in crevices and caves and among broken rocks. Built mostly of seaweed. 2-6 eggs, normally 3, length 2½ in., chalky white deposit on blue. Both sexes incubate 4 weeks : both feed young unknown period, should prove to be about 5 weeks : nestling brown, soon covered brown down (paler than cormorant). Young probably does not breed until third season after that in which it is hatched.

DISTRIBUTION. Subspecies *Phalacrocorax a. aristotelis* : from west of White Sea and Iceland south along coasts to Portugal. Feeds, and stays, within sight of rocky shores : roosts in caves and on sheltered ledges. Inland only storm-driven.

MOVEMENTS. Most shags highly resident and stay near breeding-place for whole of life. Some disperse, however, in winter to a considerable distance, though in no particular direction.

TO READ. G. A. Steven (1933). *The food consumed by shags and cormorants around the shores of Cornwall (England).* Journal of the Marine Biological Association, vol. 19, pp. 277-92. David Lack (1945). *The ecology of closely related species with special reference to cormorant* (Phalacrocorax carbo) *and shag* (P. Aristotelis). Journal of Animal Ecology, vol. 14, pp. 12–16.

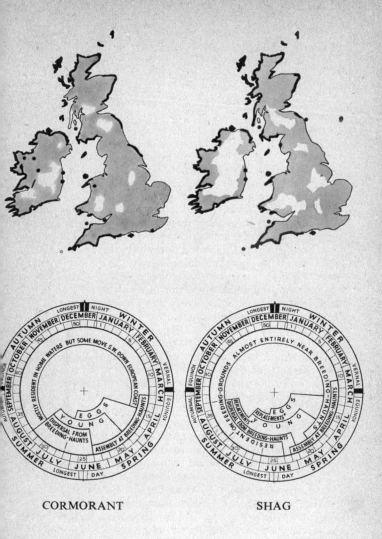

CORMORANT SHAG

Note how the maps show the cormorant to be a much more inland species than the shag.

* In the chart "replacements" mean eggs, or the young which result from eggs, that have been laid when the normal clutch or brood has been lost.

GANNET *Sula bassana* (LINNAEUS) 1758.

RECOGNITION. Very large—the largest British sea-bird. Length about 3 ft., wing-spread 6 ft., weight about $7\frac{1}{2}$ lb. Body in flight cigar-shaped : black ends to wings, rest of plumage in adults white with yellow on head, in young blackish speckled with white, black gradually lost in four years of youth : powerful bluish-white bill : legs black-brown with green lines. Plunges when fishing from height of up to 140 ft., nearly always stays under water for at least 5 seconds. Flight graceful and stately ; regular, rather rapid wing-beats with occasional glides. Feeds mainly on fish (flat-fish rarely). Voice a hoarse " arrah," at breeding-place and sometimes when fishing.

BREEDING. Social. Bowing and bill-scissoring display on breeding-grounds throughout season. Nests generally on broad ledges on steep cliffs, sometimes on tops of cliffs, built mainly of seaweed. Normally one egg, very occasionally two, length 3 in., bluish-white, becomes stained brown. Both sexes incubate, period 6 weeks or more : both feed young for 9 weeks or more : nestling black, slightly downy : later clad in white down : finally mottled black : young left by parents for about 4 weeks living on reserves of fat before fishing for itself. Young probably does not breed until fourth season after that in which it is hatched.

DISTRIBUTION. North Atlantic only, where about 166,000 breeding adults in 22 colonies in 1939 : 12 of these colonies, about 109,000 adults, in British Isles. Nearly all colonies on remote. rocky islands. Feeds usually in off-shore waters out to about the 100-fathom line. Found inland only after bad weather. Abroad, breeds in Faeroes (1 colony), Iceland (3 colonies), the Gulf of St. Lawrence and Newfoundland (6 colonies); on American side Atlantic young south to Gulf of Mexico : adults normally disperse from south Greenland to U.S. coast.

MOVEMENTS. Migrant only when young, particularly in first year, when definite passage along European coast to and from north-west Africa. Adults disperse in winter : do not normally go as far as Africa : found mainly in waters from Spain to northern Norway, and from the Rockall Bank on the west to the entrance of the Baltic on the east.

TO READ. J. H. Gurney (1913). *The gannet. A bird with a history.* London. A. Landsborough Thomson (1939). *The migration of the gannet : results of marking in the British Isles.* British Birds, vol. 32, pp. 282-9. James Fisher and H. G. Vevers (1943-4). *The breeding distribution, history and population of the North Atlantic gannet* (Sula bassana). Journal of Animal Ecology, vol. 12, pp. 173-213, vol. 13, pp. 49-62.

GANNET, about 1/12

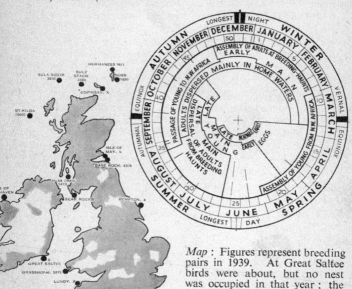

Map : Figures represent breeding pairs in 1939.   At Great Saltee birds were about, but no nest was occupied in that year ; the places marked × are the sites of extinct colonies.

STORM-PETREL *Hydrobates pelagicus* (LINNAEUS) 1758.

RECOGNITION. Very small—the smallest British sea-bird. Length about 6 in. Like a marine house-martin; sooty-black except for white rump, but square tail. Flutters like a bat. Follows ships. Feeds on surface plankton. Voice a continuous churring, only at breeding-place, mainly at night, underground.

BREEDING. Social. Display consists of chase-flights at night, when special call used ; flight in swift circles, not fluttering. Nests in burrows, natural or excavated, deep crevices in rocks, dry-stone walls. Little lining-material. Normally 1 egg, very occasionally 2, length about 1 in., white, a few brown speckles. Both sexes incubate, period 5 to 6 weeks ; both feed young 8 to 9 weeks. Nestling grey, very downy. Occupied nests are normally entered during hours of darkness; can sometimes be detected by their musty smell. Young probably does not breed until second season after that in which it is hatched.

DISTRIBUTION. Restricted to N.E. Atlantic and Mediterranean. Chain of colonies South Iceland—Faeroes—Britain—France and Channel Is.—Spain—Canaries : and into Mediterranean as far east as Malta. Inland only storm-driven.

MOVEMENTS. Winter dispersal into open Atlantic waters may carry them as far west as North American coast, and south to south-west Africa. Mediterranean birds may reach Red Sea.

TO READ. *Notes in* British Birds *on breeding-habits :* A. Gordon (1920-21), vol. 13, pp. 232-4 and vol. 14, p. 175 ; S. Gordon (1931), vol. 24, pp. 245-8 ; R. M. Lockley (1932), vol. 25, pp. 206-11.

Note : Breeding distribution on map appears as chain of colonies along oceanic islands and coasts of west Britain. Only east coast breeding record, Bass Rock, dates from 1904 ; probably not breeding now. Year-cycle chart shows lateness of egg-laying, some young still In nest October.

STORM-PETREL, about 1/3

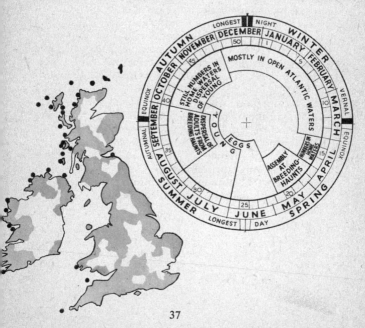

LEACH'S FORK-TAILED PETREL

Oceanodroma leucorrhoa (VIEILLOT) 1817.

RECOGNITION. Small. Length about 8 in. Black with white rump and markedly forked tail. Markedly larger than storm-petrel; bill more massive. Seldom flutters; flight buoyant, darts and glides. Does *not* follow ships. Feeds on surface plankton. Voice only at night ; on wing at breeding-place has been written " her kitti-werke-kek-ek-eroo " ; from burrow is rising and falling crooning churring.

BREEDING. Social. Display consists of excited dashing flights of birds, calling, over breeding-places, after sunset. Birds may collide in mid-air. Males stated to do all excavation of burrow ; when this is completed said to call to females who reply from air while fluttering over colony. Mating takes place in burrow whence for one night only in year is heard special mating trill, written as " mmmm, mmmmmm-mm." Nest in burrows, natural or excavated, deep crevices in rocks, dry-stone walls, ruins, lined moss and grass. One egg, length $1\frac{1}{4}$ in., white, a few sandy speckles. Both sexes incubate in turns lasting 4 to 6 days for 6 to over 7 weeks ; both feed young 7 weeks ; young finally left by parents living on reserves of fat before finding its own way to sea one night. Nestling grey, very downy. Young has adult plumage in first season after that in which it is hatched.

DISTRIBUTION. The most oceanic bird of the North Atlantic. Breeds off the coast of Maine, U.S.A. (on islands in the Bay of Fundy), in Labrador, South Greenland, the Westmann Islands (S. Iceland), Myggenaes (Faeroes), and at 4 (? 5) stations in N.W. Britain (now)—see map where from E. to W. are marked North Rona, about 380 pairs ; Sula Sgeir, about 400 pairs ; Oigh Sgeir, where one found in hole but no egg 1939 ; Flannans, about 200 pairs ; St. Kilda, about 1,000 pairs. May also breed some oceanic rocks Ireland. Also found in North Pacific. Inland in Britain only storm-driven.

MOVEMENTS. Winter dispersal into open Atlantic waters, where appear to concentrate in certain zones ; may penetrate regions south of Equator.

TO READ. J. A. Ainslie and R. Atkinson (1937). *On the breeding habits of Leach's fork-tailed petrel.* British Birds, vol. 30, pp. 234-48 and 276-7. R. Atkinson and J. A. Ainslie (1940). *The British breeding status of Leach's fork-tailed petrel.* British Birds, vol. 34, pp. 50-5. D. R. Griffin (1940). *Homing experiments with Leach's petrels.* The Auk, vol. 57, pp. 61-74.

LEACH'S FORK-TAILED PETREL, about 2/5

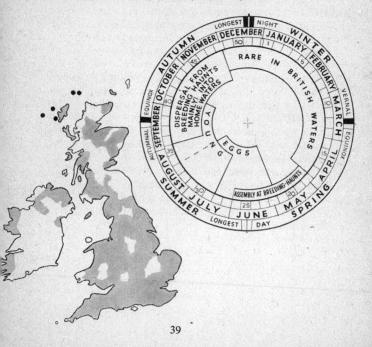

MANX SHEARWATER

Puffinus puffinus (BRÜNNICH) 1764.

RECOGNITION. Small-medium. Length about 14 in. Long narrow wings. Bill dark, hooked at tip. Black above; underparts white. Legs and feet pink and black. Flight rapid, tilting from side to side so as to appear to " shear water." Does *not* follow ships. Feeds on small fish, young fish and small squids which takes at or near surface from flight; occasionally dives, using wings to swim under water. Voice a crowing, has been written " puk-kuk-kuk-oo," mainly at breeding-place at night but recorded from " rafts " at sea and from cliffs where no breeding colony. " Rafts " are great, calm evening assemblies of shearwaters on surface of sea near breeding-grounds. Manx shearwater rises from land with great difficulty and is extremely clumsy when not in air; all traffic to and from breeding-grounds is conducted at night when there is less danger from predators, *e.g.* large gulls.

BREEDING. Social. Display seems to be mainly in burrows, with scissoring of bills. Both sexes excavate burrow, and mate in it. Burrows mostly on islands but sometimes on slopes mainland cliffs; nest lined grass and roots. One egg, length about 2½ in., white. Both sexes incubate in turns lasting 1 to 6 days for 7 to 8 weeks; both feed young 8 or 9 weeks; young finally left by parents living on reserves of fat 10 days to fortnight before scrambling to sea one night. Nestling grey-brown and grey-white, very downy. Young has adult plumage in first season after that in which it is hatched.

DISTRIBUTION. Breeds in chain of North Atlantic colonies, mainly on islands, Westmanns (S. Iceland)—Faeroes—north and west Britain (see map)—islands off France—Madeira—Azores—Bermuda. Different subspecies of same species in Mediterranean. Feed usually in offshore waters out to about the 100-fathom line. *Not* an oceanic bird. Inland only storm-driven.

MOVEMENTS. Desertion of home waters in winter is due to a southward movement mainly to the region of the Bay of Biscay.

TO READ. R. M. Lockley (1942). " Shearwaters," London, Dent.

MANX SHEARWATER, about 1/10

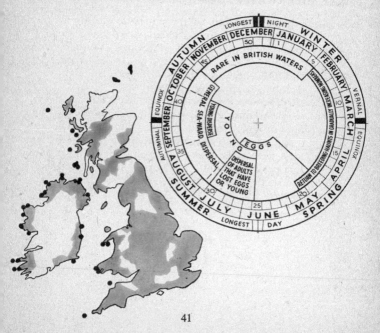

GREAT SHEARWATER

Puffinus gravis (O'REILLY) 1818.

GREAT SHEARWATER, about 1/10

RECOGNITION. Medium. Length about 18 in. Long narrow wings. Bill dark, hooked at tip. Dark brown above ; under-parts white : has more white than Manx shearwater ; on neck the white nearly meets across nape, bird thus appears to have dark-brown cap. White patch, narrow, also at base of tail, not amounting to white rump : legs and feet whitish-brown. Flight like Manx shearwater though even better at gliding. Follows fishing-boats, and eats offal ; otherwise mainly squids ; does not take food from flight but lands on water; can dive from surface and swim under water with wings. Voice has been heard when feeding, harsh ; other shearwaters feed silently.

DISTRIBUTION. Known only to breed on islands in Tristan da Cunha group in South Atlantic.

MOVEMENTS. A southern hemisphere breeder which visits the North Atlantic in its off-season (our summer). Disperses throughout North Atlantic, where abundant Newfoundland Banks and reaches Greenland and Iceland. In Britain visits Hebrides, west coast Ireland, Devon and Cornwall, and sometimes east coast England ; inland only storm-driven.

TO READ. H. F. Witherby (1940). *The species of great shearwaters in the English Channel.* British Birds, vol. 33, pp. 248-9.

SOOTY SHEARWATER
Puffinus griseus (Gmelin) 1879.

SOOTY SHEARWATER, about 1/5

RECOGNITION. Medium. Length about 16 in. Wings appear very long and narrow. Bill dark, hooked at tip. Entirely sooty-black except for pale line under wing. Legs and feet blackish. Flight, food and feeding habits like great shearwater; swims slowly under water with wings. Voice not recorded away from breeding-grounds.

DISTRIBUTION. Breeds on islands and coasts of New Zealand and southern South America.

MOVEMENTS. A southern hemisphere breeder which visits the North Atlantic and North Pacific in its off-season (our summer). Disperses throughout North Atlantic as great shearwater, but range in seas round British coasts (where a good deal rarer) slightly different; found most usually off Forth, N.E. England, Kent, Cornwall, Pembrokeshire, S.W. Ireland and Hebrides; inland only storm-driven.

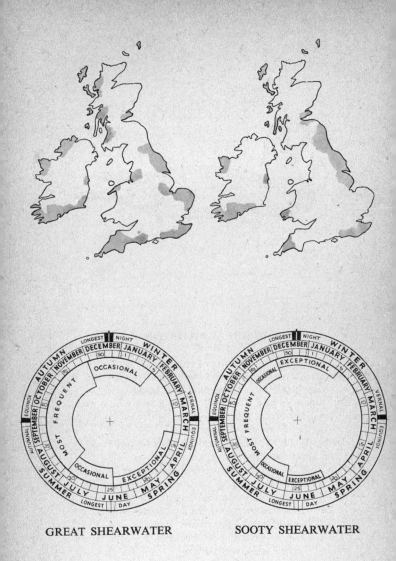

GREAT SHEARWATER   **SOOTY SHEARWATER**

FULMAR *Fulmarus glacialis* (LINNAEUS) 1761.

FULMAR, about 1/6

RECOGNITION. Medium. Length about 18 in. Grey above, yellow-white underparts ; or entirely grey-blue. No black tips to wings. Whitish patch near tip of wings. Fairly short heavy bill with prominent tubular nostrils, colour variable. Legs and feet bluish. At a distance has the appearance of a gull, but the flight of a shearwater; a magnificent glider. In flight head streamlines with body without any apparent " neck " between. Lands on water to feed, occasionally up-ends, but does not swim under water. Eats oily offal, blubber, any oily matter it can get ; but chiefly surface plankton, including large amount of jelly-fish ; and a small amount of fish. Follows ships. Occasionally grunts on water or in air, but voice chiefly heard on breeding-cliffs, " ag-ag-ag-ag-arrrr."

The " blue," or " dark " forms of the fulmar are very rare indeed among the birds at any breeding-colony south or west of Bear Island or Spitsbergen. In autumn and winter they come south from the arctic and are not rare in the North Sea.

BREEDING. Social. Displays from November to August, on sea by breeding-cliffs but mainly on nesting-place. Often three birds take part ; puff out skin of throat, open beak wide to show conspicuous pale green interior, and move head from side to side uttering voice. Nibble and lock bills. Typically nests on oceanic cliffs, but in Spitsbergen on cliffs up to 20 miles

W368   45

from sea ; in Britain where originally only bred oceanic cliffs
has now penetrated to sheltered coasts and has bred six miles
from open sea in Northumberland. Normal nest-site on
steep grassy slope above high cliffs, but also nests among broken
rocks, on ruins and houses, screes, sand-dunes and banks,
and in semi-burrows. Nest material none, or scanty grass and
pebbles. Normally 1 egg, very exceptionally 2, never replaced
when destroyed, length 3 in., white. Both parents incubate
in turns lasting about 4 days for 6 to 8 weeks ; both feed young
6 to 8 weeks ; young finally left by parents for week to 10 days
living on reserves of fat before flying to sea. Nestling grey and
white ; very thick down. Young apparently has adult plumage
in first season after that in which it is hatched.

DISTRIBUTION. Two subspecies, in N. Pacific and N.
Atlantic. N. Atlantic subspecies *F. g. glacialis* occupied chain of
breeding colonies—Lonely Island—Novaya Zemlya—Franz
Josef Land—Spitsbergen—N.E. Greenland—Bear Island—Jan
Mayen—E. Greenland—Iceland—St. Kilda (with outposts in W.
Greenland and Baffin Land) until 1820, when breeding range
began to increase in Iceland ; between 1816 and 1839 spread to
Faeroes, where now abundant ; in 1878 spread to Shetland and
has continued to spread in Britain until present day (see map) ;
in 1924 spread to Norway ; may by now have spread to France.
In ordinary inland areas is a storm-driven accidental visitor.

MOVEMENTS. Winter dispersal into Atlantic and North
Sea, mixes the arctic and sub-arctic populations. Northern limit
of oceanic distribution is the sea-ice at all seasons. Does not often
go further south
than 40 degrees lati-
tude or into regions
of a temperature
consistently more
than 60 degrees F.

TO READ. James
Fisher and George
Waterston (1941). *The
breeding distribution,
history and population
of the fulmar* (Ful-
marus glacialis) *in the
British Isles.* Journal
of Animal Ecology,
vol. 10, pp. 204-72.

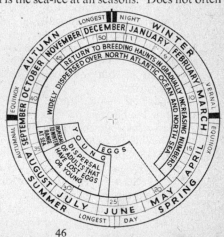

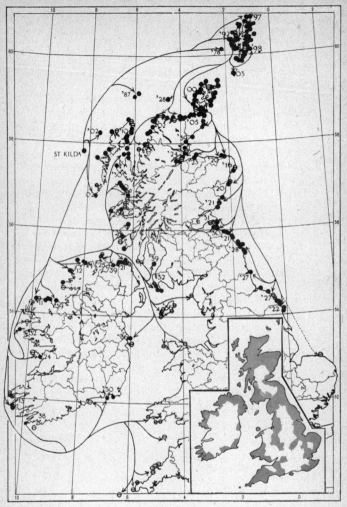

Map showing the main directions of the spread of the breeding fulmar in Britain (supposing that it originated at St. Kilda) and the colonies in 1939. Black dots are breeding colonies, " open " dots places where birds were, by 1939, showing interest in cliffs, etc., but were not yet breeding. Figures represent the dates at which breeding was first definitely established in each vice-county. (*Inset:* Non-breeding occurrences).

BAR-TAILED GODWIT
Limosa lapponica (LINNAEUS) 1758.

RECOGNITION. Small-medium. Length 14 in. without bill. Bill about 4 in., noticeably upcurved. Legs grey, only project slightly beyond tail in flight. General colour mottled brown-grey in winter (see p. 175) ; in breeding season male assumes beautiful rufous plumage. No wing-bar. Rump dull white. tail barred (looks dirty white in field view). Under-parts whiter than curlew ; breast only faintly streaked. Neck appears short in flight. Birds often glide some distance before pitching. Feeds, largely by probing in mud with long bill, on insects, worms, crustaceans and molluscs. Voice rare away from breeding grounds but " kirruc " sometimes heard from birds in flocks.

DISTRIBUTION. Breeds in arctic Europe and Siberia. Visits Britain on passage and in winter ; and a few non-breeders stay in summer. Keeps mainly to coastal areas, and is rare in Northern Highlands and anywhere inland. Passage continues along Atlantic cost to Africa, and through Mediterranean and Red Sea coasts to Gulf of Aden. Nearly reaches equator.

MOVEMENTS. Autumn passage migrants from Scandinavia seem mostly to strike Britain between Morayshire and Aberdeenshire, and work south thence down east coast. A few pass from Shetland to the Hebrides and down the west coasts of Scotland and Ireland. Some of the east coast passengers cross over the Lowlands to the west and pass down the east coast of Ireland, and the west coast of England. Return passage in spring is mostly up east coast.

TO READ. F. W. Holder and R. Wagstaffe (1930). *The migrations of the bar-tailed godwit as observed on the South Lancashire coast.* British Birds, vol. 23, pp. 318-23.

BAR-TAILED GODWIT, summer plumage, about 1/5 (for winter plumage see p. 175)

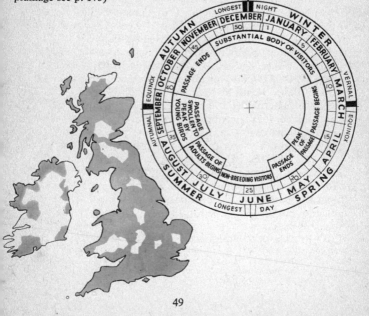

BLACK-TAILED GODWIT

Limosa limosa (LINNAEUS) 1758.

RECOGNITION. Medium. Length 16 in. without bill. Bill *over* 4 in., only faintly upcurved. Legs green-black, project beyond tail in flight and longer than bar-tailed godwit's. General colour dark mottled brown-grey in winter (see p. 175) ; in breeding season male assumes rufous plumage but on breast only ; belly and under-tail remain whitish. *Broad white wing-bar*. Rump dark but tail pure white with broad black band near tip. Under-parts in winter light grey, not as white as bar-tailed godwit's ; back brown-grey, darker and more uniform than other godwit's. Neck appears short in flight. May wade quite deeply and feeds by probing on insects, worms, crustaceans, molluscs, fish and amphibians. Voice heard from birds in flocks " wicka-wicka-wicka " ; other notes on breeding-grounds.

BREEDING. Solitary. Male has display-flight, mounts to height, does rolling flight followed by glide and sudden pitch, calling " tur-ee-tur " and then " grutto." Male also struts round female on ground with tail expanded and tilted ; also does ceremonial scraping. Nest usually on water-meadows or in marshes, sometimes beneath a bush ; lined grass and down. 3-5 eggs, normally 4, length $2\frac{1}{4}$ in., greenish, usually spotted brown. Both sexes incubate in turn $3\frac{1}{2}$ weeks ; both feed young. Nestling leaves nest as soon as it can run, very long-legged, chestnut-buff with dark markings. Young does not get full adult plumage until second season after that in which it is hatched.

DISTRIBUTION. Not an arctic species. Breeds in Europe south of Baltic, south Sweden and Iceland. Used to breed fairly widely in eastern England, 100 years ago, but now very exceptional breeder (has lately bred Lincs.). Another subspecies of same species in northern Asia. European birds pass through Mediterranean region to winter in Africa, occasionally beyond equator.

MOVEMENTS. Has increased in England in last 40 years and besides passage migrants, many now stay for winter and a few for summer. Is fairly common inland, especially at sewage-farms, on passage. Autumn passage mainly along south coast England, but has developed in East Anglia and the Mersey area in last 30 years.

TO READ. J. S. Huxley and F. A. Montague (1926). *Studies on the courtship and sexual life of birds*, VI. *The black-tailed godwit*, Limosa limosa (L.). Ibis, series 12, vol. 2, pp. 1-25. Miss A. Morley (1930). *The black-tailed godwit in the British Isles*, 1890-1937. British Birds, vol. 33, pp. 98-104.

BLACK-TAILED GODWIT, summer plumage, about 1/6 (for winter plumage see p. 175)

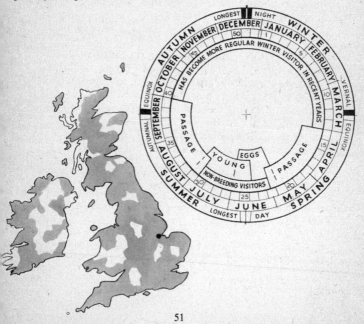

CURLEW Numenius arquata (LINNAEUS) 1758.

RECOGNITION. Medium. Length nearly 2 ft. without bill. Bill very long, about 5 in., strongly down-curved. Streaky brown plumage with no distinctive pattern on crown. Very shy. Flight heavy for a wader ; normally glides in for some distance to pitch ; neck appears short and downcurved bill visible at considerable distance. May wade quite deeply and feeds by probing on molluscs, worms, insects, crustaceans, fish and amphibians. Also eats berries. Casts pellets and, from time to time, the lining of its gizzard. Voice very different from whimbrel's ; normally " croo-ee," other notes on breeding-grounds.

BREEDING. Solitary. In display male glides with trembling wings and utters famous trill, a crescendo of bubbling notes. On ground males lift wings vertically to show white under-sides and pairs may play leap-frog. Nests in grass fields, water meadows, marshes and moors. Nest usually lined grass. Eggs 3-6, normally 4, length 2¾ in., green-brown with small brown spots. Both sexes incubate in turns 4 weeks or more, both parents tend young which can fly in 5 weeks or 6. Nestling sandy, with many dark brown markings. Young does not quite get full adult plumage until second season after that in which it is hatched.

· DISTRIBUTION. Breeds from arctic Europe (not Iceland) to northern France, east to borders of Europe. Another sub-species of same species in Asia. Spreading as a breeding species in England. May winter anywhere between breeding-place and S. Africa, some staying on coast near breeding-grounds.

MOVEMENTS. In Britain big movement of Scottish and English birds to Ireland in autumn. Continental birds work along east and south coasts England, and overland to Ireland. Return by same routes.

TO READ. R. H. Brown (1939). *Notes on the lapwing and curlew breeding populations of a Cumberland farm.* British Birds, vol. 33, pp. 12-15. Miss A. Hibbert-Ware and R. F. Ruttledge (1944). *A study of the inland food habits of the common curlew.* British Birds, vol. 38, pp. 22-7.

CURLEW, about 1/8

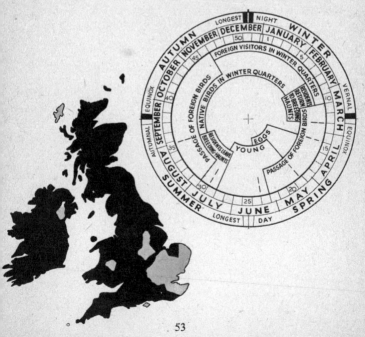

WHIMBREL *Numenius phaeopus* (LINNAEUS) 1758.

RECOGNITION. Small-medium. Length about 15 in. without bill, bill a little over 3 in. Bill not so long or curved as curlew's. Streaky brown plumage with two dark bands on crown and pale streak between. Tamer than curlew. Flight like curlew's only wing-beats more rapid. Feeds by probing on insects, worms, molluscs, spiders. Also eats berries. Voice normally a trilling titter, usually of seven beats, quite unmistakable and unique.

BREEDING. Solitary. In display male glides with bubbling song much like that of curlew ; also tumbling flight. Nests on moorland in Britain, open, usually lined grass. Eggs 3-5, normally 4, length $2\frac{1}{4}$ in., green-brown with dark spots. Both parents incubate about $3\frac{1}{2}$ weeks ; both tend young which flies at about 4 weeks. Nestling like curlew's but lighter and less sandy in colour. Young does not quite get full adult plumage until second season after that in which it is hatched.

DISTRIBUTION. Breeds in arctic and sub-arctic ; in Siberia, Russia, Scandinavia, Iceland, Faeroes and N. Britain. In N. Britain very small numbers breed, and does not breed all areas marked on map every year. In winter reaches S. Africa and S. Arabia.

MOVEMENTS. Passage often at night, apparently high ; can be detected (as can passage of curlew) by call. Sometimes heard over London. Main movement in Britain along all coasts, but quite frequent inland. Whimbrel is strict passage-migrant and quite exceptional in winter and (apart from few breeders) in summer in British Isles. Seems to be more often noticed in spring than in autumn. Large stream through Hebrides.

TO READ. W. E. Glegg (1923). *A note on the nesting of the whimbrel.* British Birds, vol. 17, pp. 70-6. R. Chislett (1923). *The whimbrel in Shetland.* British Birds, vol. 17, pp. 150-4. A. H. Daukes (1931). *Breeding of the whimbrel in Inverness-shire.* British Birds, vol. 25, pp. 62-5.

WHIMBREL, about 1/5

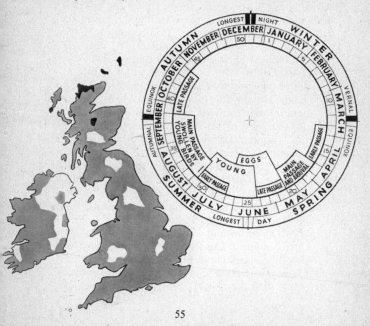

WOODCOCK Scolopax rusticola LINNAEUS 1758.

RECOGNITION. Small-medium. Length about 14-in. without bill ; bill about 3 in., very long and straight. Bird has stout build with a rich " marbled " plumage pattern on back. Rises without voice but often a wing-clap ; wings appear rounded in flight ; a woodland species. When put up by day dodges round trees in flight but in open flies straight. Feeds mainly at dawn and dusk often at feeding-grounds outside its wood, to which it " flights " ; probes in soft ground with bill ; chief food is earthworms but also eats insects, spiders, molluscs, crustaceans and seeds. Voice seldom heard except during roding or other display.

BREEDING. Solitary. In display, at dusk and dawn, male goes roding, which consists of flying a particular circuit of its wood above the trees, uttering a note like " whick," with a good deal of whistle to it, and also croaking a gentle, repeated groan. As it croaks it appears to check and lose a wing-beat. Display also on ground of the familiar " wader " type in which male arches wings, spreads tail and faces female. Nest is hollow on ground in wood lined with leaves. Eggs 3-6, normally 4, length $1\frac{3}{4}$ in., buff spotted warm brown. Female alone incubates about 3 weeks and tends young for unknown period during which she may carry them in flight between her legs or, very exceptionally, on her back. Two broods. Nestling russet and buff ; highly cryptic (hiding) pattern of colours. Young gets adult plumage in first season after that in which it is hatched.

DISTRIBUTION. Breeds throughout Europe and Asia, though not in high arctic or Iceland, or in hotter Mediterranean countries. In Britain does not breed Anglesey, or normally in Pembrokeshire and Cornwall, and rarely in west country, west Wales and midlands, or north isles ; otherwise regular breeder everywhere. Winters in summer haunts or migrates ; many migrants reach Mediterranean shores and tropical Asia.

MOVEMENTS. South of Mersey and Humber all British breeders appear to be resident. So are most Irish breeders. Woodcock that breed in N. England and Scotland show partial migration ; tend to be truly stationary or definitely migratory. Of the migrants, most go to Ireland, some to S. England and some to France, Spain and Portugal. Migrants also arrive in autumn from continent, and pass mainly by east and west coasts, though also overland. Those passing by the west mostly go to Ireland. Spring migration seems to be a simple reversal.

TO READ. W. B. Alexander (1945-6). *The woodcock in the British Isles.* Ibis, vol. 87, pp. 512-50 ; vol. 88, pp. 1-24, 271-86, 427-44.

WOODCOCK, about 1/6

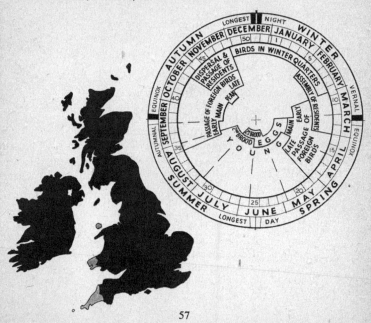

SNIPE   *Capella gallinago* (LINNAEUS) 1758.

RECOGNITION. Small.   Length about 8 in. without bill. Bill 2½ in., very long and straight, clearly visible when bird in flight. Bird has finer build than woodcock and plumage pattern gives barred rather than marbled impression. Pale central stripes on crown. Rises with hoarse note and zig-zag flight ; wings appear pointed in flight ; a marsh and meadow species. Feeds mainly at dawn and dusk ; probes in mud for worms ; also eats insects, molluscs, crustaceans and seeds. Utters hoarse " scape " when flushed. Quite often perches off the ground. Often social in winter, forming flocks up to 100.

BREEDING. Solitary. Display by both sexes includes a vocal song, " chipper, chipper, chipper " which has the rhythm of a piston, and the well-known drumming, which is instrumental. During dive, outer pair of tail-feathers is held nearly at right-angles to direction of flight, and rush of air past and through these causes a humming sound. Males also have usual " wader " display to females on ground with arched wings and expanded tail. Nest in water meadows and moor-bogs, often in tussock, lined with grass. Eggs 3-6, normally 4, length about 1½ in., brown spots on olive. Female alone incubates for 3 weeks or nearly 3 weeks ; both parents tend young for unknown period. Sometimes two broods. Nestling tawny and black, highly cryptic. Young gets adult plumage in first season after that in which it is hatched.

DISTRIBUTION. In Europe and Asia much as woodcock, though breeds further north (well into arctic) and somewhat further south (*e.g.*, in Spain and Portugal). Extends in winter to equatorial regions Africa and Asia. *Capella gallinago faeroensis,* the snipe of Iceland and the Faeroes, breeds also in Orkney and Shetland where it replaces *C. g. gallinago*, the snipe of the rest of Britain and Europe. In Britain common everywhere.

MOVEMENTS. Much the same as in woodcock. South of Mersey and Humber all British breeders appear to be resident. North of this there is a *partial* migration to Ireland in winter. No evidence yet that British breeders are ever found outside the British Isles. Migrants arrive in autumn from the continent ; these behave much as do the corresponding woodcock. Those passing along north-west coast route mostly go to Ireland, those along east coast to S. England or countries beyond.

TO READ. J. W. Seigne and E. C. Keith (1936). *Woodcock and Snipe*. London, Philip Allan.

SNIPE, about 1/4

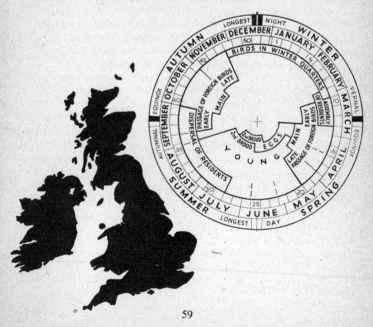

JACK SNIPE   *Lymnocryptes minimus* (BRÜNNICH) 1764.

RECOGNITION. Very small. Length about 7 in. without bill. Bill 1½ in., well visible in flight but relatively shorter than that of snipe. Bird is snipe-like with dark plumage (no white on tail) and rich pattern of stripes giving mottled impression rather than barred as in snipe. Two pale stripes over eye separated by narrow black stripe. Rises reluctantly, usually silently and with slower and straighter flight than snipe ; a marsh and bog species. Probes with bill for worms ; also eats molluscs, insects and seeds. Voice seldom heard in Britain, but in display over or on breeding-ground makes vocal sound like galloping horse. Solitary, even in winter, and nearly always rises alone.

DISTRIBUTION. Breeds in northern Europe, from well in to the arctic (not Iceland) to the south shores of the Baltic, and in northern Asia. Migrates in winter to beyond the Sahara in Africa and as far as Ceylon in Asia. In Britain is a passage-migrant and winter visitor, widely spread in small numbers. Is probably more widely spread in Ireland than map indicates. Map probably shows lack of observers in Ireland rather than lack of jack snipe.

MOVEMENTS. Passage through Britain takes place inland, but mostly along normal coastal routes ; along east coasts Scotland and England and thence along south coast England; and through Hebrides dividing into routes down west coast Ireland, east coast Ireland and west coast England and Wales.

TO READ. Ralph Chislett (1927). *Notes on the breeding of the jack snipe*. British Birds, vol. 21, pp. 2-6.

JACK SNIPE, about 1/3

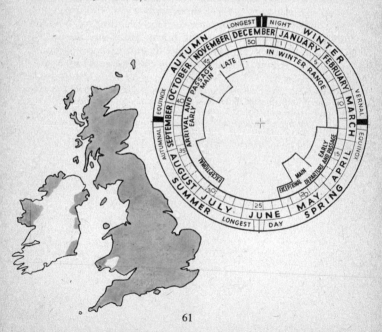

GREY PHALAROPE

Phalaropus fulicarius (LINNAEUS) 1758.

RECOGNITION. Small. Length about 8 in. Yellow bill with black tip, shorter and broader than red-necked phalarope's. In summer all under-parts chestnut and sides of face whitish, back striped brown, buff and chestnut. Female brighter than male in breeding plumage. In winter (p. 176) very difficult to distinguish from red-necked phalarope and not always easy to tell from sanderling. Size not much help. Bill size and shape helps. Back is grey, more uniform than red-necked phalarope's, and white wing-bar less prominent. Both phalaropes in winter have dark streak through eye which sanderling lacks ; also have much more slender bodies ; and sanderling never swims. Grey phalarope swims buoyantly and " spins " on water at breeding grounds and in open sea. Flight swift, in usual small wader style. Feeds on crustaceans, molluscs, insects and worms on or near surface of water, while swimming, also on land like sanderling or dunlin. Also eats seeds. Voice " whit." Solitary at breeding-grounds but often social outside breeding-season. Very tame.

DISTRIBUTION AND MOVEMENTS. An arctic breeder, by pools in the tundra throughout islands and shores of Polar Basin, including Iceland but not northern Scandinavia. Winters *at sea* in southern hemisphere, off coasts Africa and S. America. On passage travels via intervening inland waters and coasts, including those of Britain, particularly coasts southern and eastern England.

TO READ. A. L. V. Manniche (1910). *The terrestrial birds and mammals of north-east Greenland ; biological observations.* Meddelelser om Grønland, vol. 45, pp. 1-200. Miss M. D. Haviland (1915). *Notes on the breeding-habits of the grey phalarope.* British Birds, vol. 9, pp. 11-16.

GREY PHALAROPE, summer plumage, about 2/5 (for winter plumage see p. 176)

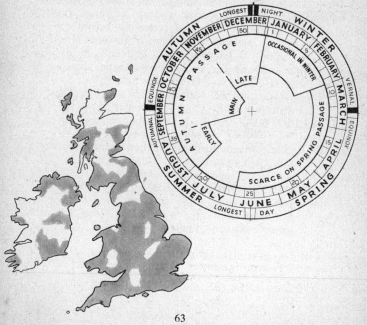

RED-NECKED PHALAROPE

Phalaropus lobatus (LINNAEUS) 1758.

RECOGNITION. Very small. Length about 6 in. Black bill, longer and finer than grey phalarope's. In summer under-parts and throat white, orange band on sides of neck and upper breast, back slate-grey. Female brighter than male in breeding-plumage. In winter (p. 176) difficult to distinguish from grey phalarope (see previous page) ; back is darker grey with whitish streaks, less uniform than grey phalarope's ; wings darker than grey phalarope's and white wing-bar more prom-inent. Swims buoyantly and " spins," a method of stirring up edible animals on water at breeding-grounds and in open sea. Feeds mainly while swimming on insects, molluscs and worms. Also eats seeds. Voice " whit " like grey phalarope's ; very hard to distinguish but said to be lower-pitched. Other notes on breeding-grounds. Social outside breeding-season. Very tame.

BREEDING. Social. Display by female ; ceremonial flight with repeated " whit-whit-whit." Female also courts male on water ; swims with lowered head, or may raise body on tail and whirr wings ; or may do usual wader " scraping " on ground which male does also. Special ceremony before egg-laying. Nests on marshy ground near water, in tussocks, lined grass. Eggs 3-5, normally 4, length about 1¼ in., buff with dark spots. Male alone incubates for about 3 weeks, and alone manages young for up to 3 weeks. Nestling has a remarkable pattern of cinnamon, black and buff stripes on top, grey-white below. It is not known how long it takes to reach maturity.

DISTRIBUTION. An arctic and sub-arctic species. Breeds all round Polar Basin ; breeding-range extends into N. Atlantic and N. Pacific. Breeds Iceland, Faeroes, Scandinavia and five places in N.W. Britain (see map). Rare inland in Britain, and rare anywhere in Ireland apart from breeding-place.

MOVEMENTS. Winters at sea as grey phalarope, but seldom reaches equator and only exceptionally penetrates beyond. European birds to West Africa. Passage touches east and south coasts of England, rarely any other part of Britain.

TO READ. P. H. Bahr (1907). *Some observations on the breeding habits of the red-necked phalarope.* British Birds, vol. 1, pp. 202-7. Miss M. G. S. Best and Miss M. D. Haviland (1914). *Notes on the red-necked phalarope in the Outer Hebrides.* British Birds, vol. 8, pp. 9-12.

RED-NECKED PHALAROPE, summer plumage, about 1/2 (for winter plumage see p. 176)

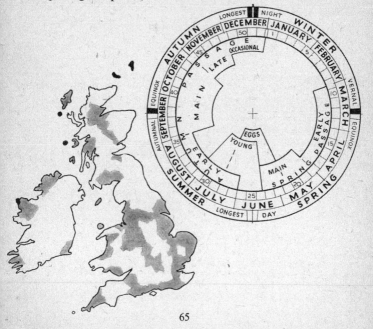

TURNSTONE *Arenaria interpres* (LINNAEUS) 1758.

RECOGNITION. Small. Length about 9 in. Conical, short, pointed, black bill, rather thick at base, slightly up-curved. Tail slightly rounded. On ground upper-parts of bird have tortoise-shell appearance. Broad dark band on breast. Bold pied pattern in flight ; white on rump clear, looks like oval patch. Legs orange. Most often found in small parties working along tidemark of rocky shores ; when put up flight appears weak, though not so when flying a distance. Feeds by turning stones (sometimes co-operating), on insects, spiders, crustaceans and molluscs, can open small mussels and limpets. Also eats small fish and seeds. Most usual voice " titititit." Social outside breeding-season and somewhat so on breeding-grounds.

DISTRIBUTION. An arctic and sub-arctic species ; breeds in Scandinavia and Baltic, northern Europe and Asia. Different sub-species in American arctic. Our subspecies again in Greenland (*A i. interpres*), and breeds occasionally in Iceland. Has never been proved to breed in Britain though many stay for summer, especially in Orkney and Shetland and on North Rona ; but regular winter visitor and passage migrant nearly all parts, especially along coasts.

MOVEMENTS. Winters up to and beyond equator, in S. Africa, Indian Ocean, Pacific and S. America. Passage through Britain by all usual coastal routes ; inland as well.

TO READ. A. H. Paget-Wilkes (1922). *On the breeding-habits of the turnstone as observed in Spitsbergen.* British Birds, vol. 15, pp. 172-9. Ralph Chislett (1925). *Turnstones on a Baltic islet.* British Birds, vol. 19, pp. 2-9, and (1935). *Northward ho !—for birds.* London, Country Life, pp. 138-47. J. M. Dewar (1940). *Identity of specialized feeding-habits of the turnstone and the oyster-catcher.* British Birds, vol. 34, pp. 26-8.

TURNSTONE, about 1/3

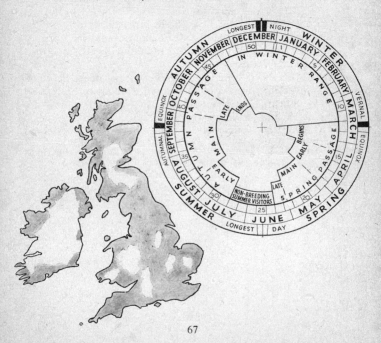

KNOT   *Calidris canutus* (LINNAEUS) 1758.

RECOGNITION. Small. Length about 10 in. Bill straight and rather short. Legs rather short. Not very conspicuous white wing-bar. White lower rump and tail with black barring appears in field as pale patch. Grey streaks on flanks. In summer breeding-dress underparts become rufous instead of white as in winter (p. 176). A stocky bird, the largest shore wader of the dunlin type ; haunts open flats in great flocks. Flight in large flocks swift ; flocks do evolutions and sometimes look like dark smoke-clouds blown by gusts. On mud and sand flock moves as one ; birds probe rapidly for crustaceans, worms and molluscs. Also eat insects, spiders and buds. Voice a low " knot," sounds musical when uttered by many in a flock. Solitary inland in Britain, and on breeding-grounds.

DISTRIBUTION. An arctic species. Breeding-grounds have only been discovered on tundra in northernmost Siberia, Spitsbergen, Greenland and some Canadian arctic islands. Birds in Greenland and to west belong to subspecies *C. c. rufa ;* rest to *C. c. canutus* which migrates in winter as far as Black Sea and N. and W. Africa, and countries round Arabian Sea. In Britain, passage migrant and winter visitor in large flocks on suitable flats along east coast Scotland and England, round the north of Ireland, and along N.W. England. Individual birds sometimes inland at sewage farms.

MOVEMENTS. Autumn stream down east coast Scotland divides, west element proceeding across Lowlands to N. Ireland and N.W. England. Otherwise use usual coastal routes, not continuing beyond Mayo on west of Ireland.

TO READ. H. W. Feilden (1920). *Breeding of the knot in Grinnell Land.* British Birds, vol. 13, pp. 278-82. C. T. Dalgety, J. H. McNeile and M. J. Ingram (1931). *Notes on birds observed in Spitsbergen during the spring of* 1930. Ibis, series 13, vol. 1, pp. 243-55.

KNOT, summer plumage, about 3/10 (for winter plumage see p. 176)

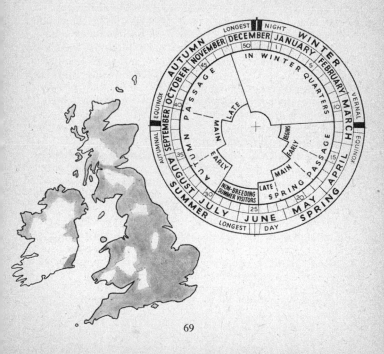

DUNLIN *Calidris alpina* (LINNAEUS) 1758.

RECOGNITION. Very small. Length about 7 in. Only slightly smaller than sanderling. Typical " round-shouldered " appearance. Black bill, fairly long, may be straight or slightly down-curved. Legs dark olive. Active runner but not as fast as sanderling. White wing-bar definite but less prominent than in sanderling. Compare carefully also with curlew-sandpiper ; best field difference is white rump of curlew-sandpiper—bill unreliable as means of detecting these species. In winter (p. 177) dunlin shows much less white than sanderling ; is brownish-grey with throat, belly and under-tail alone white. In summer mantle becomes chestnut and black, and black patch develops on lower breast. In winter haunts beaches and open flats, in flocks, often large. Flocks do aerial evolutions. In feeding finds molluscs and worms by sight and touch in sand and mud ; sometimes swallows animals while bill still probing sand. Food includes insects, molluscs, crustaceans and worms. Voice away from breeding-ground " turr " in flocks, sometimes " two-up " or " twerp " when flushed.

BREEDING. Solitary. Male, and possibly also female, has display-flight, with hovering and gliding during which bird utters a rising trill. Wing-lifting to expose white under-side also observed. Nests on coastal marshes and moorland ; in tussock, lined woody stems and leaves. Eggs 2-6, normally 4, length up to $1\frac{1}{2}$ in., green-buff, spotted and blotched brown. Both sexes incubate for 3 weeks or more. Hen does most management of young which fly between 3 and 4 weeks after hatching. Nestling has cryptic pattern on back of yellow, buff and black ; white underneath. Young practically gets adult plumage, and may breed in first season after that in which it is hatched.

DISTRIBUTION. Two subspecies in Britain. British breeder is *C. a. schinzii*, the southern dunlin, which, outside Britain, breeds all round the Baltic, and in the Faeroes and Iceland ; and migrates as far as N. Africa. *C. a. alpina*, the northern dunlin (larger) breeds in arctic Europe and Siberia and reaches much further on migration—S. Africa and India. Very few southern dunlins stay in Britain, but many northern birds winter here, so in effect we exchange one subspecies for the other each season.

MOVEMENTS. Both subspecies pass along normal coastal routes as well as by land in autumn and spring.

TO READ. R. H. Brown (1938). *Breeding-habits of the dunlin*. British Birds, vol. 31, pp. 362-6.

DUNLIN, summer plumage, about 2/5 (for winter plumage see p. 177)

CURLEW-SANDPIPER

Calidris testacea (PALLAS) 1764.

RECOGNITION. Very small. Length about 7 in. Bill down-curved, longish and fine. Compare carefully with dunlin ; bill is *not* safe means of distinction. Safe distinction is rump, clear white in curlew-sandpiper. Curlew-sandpiper's legs longer than dunlin's. Fairly conspicuous white wing-bar. In winter plum-age (p. 177) contrast of grey and white upper- and under-sides is more clear than in dunlin. Mixed flocks of dunlin and curlew-sandpipers are fairly common and in them it is possible to dis-tinguish the "chirrup" of the curlew-sandpiper from the "turr" of the dunlin. Breeding plumage is chestnut, like knot, on breast and belly. Flies and feeds as, and often with, dunlin ; eats crustaceans, molluscs, worms, insects and seeds.

DISTRIBUTION AND MOVEMENTS. Breeds in arctic Asia, and migrates across equator to S. Africa, India and Australasia, sometimes down to southern S. America. In Britain a passage migrant only. Main stream in autumn arrives north-eastern Scotland and divides, part continuing down normal east coast route, and part crossing Scotland or N. England (in which regions bird most often recorded inland) to proceed down west coast England and Wales. Of the western passengers a few pass along coasts of N.E. Ireland. Few birds use west route on spring return.

TO READ. Miss M. D. Haviland (1915). *Notes on the breeding-habits of the curlew-sandpiper*. British Birds, vol. 8, pp. 178-83.

CURLEW-SANDPIPER, summer plumage, about 2/5 (for winter. plumage see p. 177)

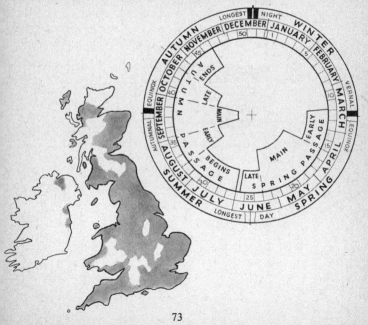

LITTLE STINT *Calidris minuta* (LEISLER) 1812.

RECOGNITION. Minute. Length under 6 in. Stints are smallest British waders. Narrow white wing-bar, not very conspicuous. Bill and legs black. In summer upper-parts mainly rufous and buff mottled black. In winter (p. 177) upper-parts ashy-brown. White feathers on back make V-mark with apex towards rump. Under-parts mainly white. Habits rather like dunlin, frequents (in Britain) sand and flats in flocks which perform evolutions. Compare with Temminck's stint. Feeds on insects, crustaceans, molluscs, earthworms and seeds. Voice away from breeding-grounds, when flushed, " chit-chit-chit." Very tame.

DISTRIBUTION AND MOVEMENTS. Breeds in arctic Europe (not Iceland or Spitsbergen) and arctic Asia. Migrates across equator as far as S. Africa and Ceylon. In Britain passage migrant only. Main stream in autumn arrives middle of east coast Scotland and proceeds down normal east coast route, thence along south coast England. Some arrive in Moray Firth area further north and appear to cross Scotland by Great Glen, filtering through inner Hebrides to N. Ireland. Main stream also gives off westerly branches which cross Scotland and N. England to travel down west coast routes. But main passage in autumn, and practically the whole of the spring return, is by east coast route.

TO READ. Miss M. D. Haviland (1915). *Notes on the breeding-habits of the little stint.* British Birds, vol. 8, pp. 202-8.

LITTLE STINT, summer plumage, about 1/2 (for winter plumage
see p. 177

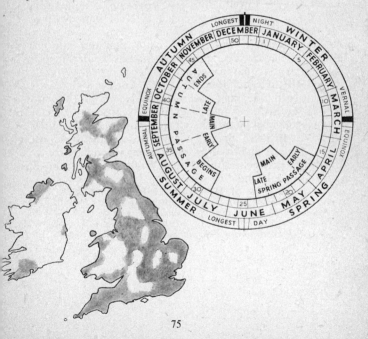

TEMMINCK'S STINT

Calidris temminckii (LEISLER) 1812.

RECOGNITION. Minute. Length under 6 in. Narrow white wing-bar not very conspicuous. Bill very dark brown, legs yellow-brown to greenish. In summer darker, duller and less rufous than little stint, and in winter (p. 177) greyer; under-parts white but definite grey breast. Outer feathers of tail white. Many habits, including fluttering type of flight, are of " common sandpiper " rather than " dunlin " type ; contrast this with little stint whose habits are dunlin-like. Flocks, for instance, are smaller than those of little stint and do not perform evolutions. Feeds by picking as much as by probing on insects and worms. Voice a trilling note quite unlike little stint's. Not as tame or social as little stint.

BREEDING. Solitary. Trill which is normal note is developed in male's display-flight, in which wings are fluttered and tail spread ; flight ends with glide. Trill and wing-fluttering may continue on ground. Also usual wing-lifting, exposing silvery under-side. Nest usually in scrub near water, lined stems or grass. Eggs 3 or 4, normally 4, length up to $1\frac{1}{4}$ in., greenish with brown spots. Both sexes incubate for unknown period. Young managed by male for about 3 weeks. Nestling rather like dunlin's with cryptic pattern yellow, buff and dark brown, grey-white underneath. Practically attains adult plumage in first season after that in which it is hatched.

DISTRIBUTION. Breeds in arctic Europe and Asia ; has recently been spreading southward in Norway. Eggs laid in Spey Valley, Scotland, in 1934 and in one year since then. Otherwise passage-migrant in Britain, much rarer than little stint.

MOVEMENTS. Species migrates to equator in Africa and Asia. Passage in Britain irregular except along southern part of normal east coast route (from Wash to south) and along south coast England.

TO READ. Miss M. D. Haviland (1916). *Notes on the breeding-habits of Temminck's stint*. British Birds, vol. 10, pp. 157-65. G. R. Edwards (1934). *Breeding of Temminck's stint in Scotland*. British Birds, vol. 28, pp. 97-9. H. N. Southern and W. A. S. Lewis (1938). *The breeding behaviour of Temminck's stint*. British Birds, vol. 31, pp. 314-21.

TEMMINCK'S STINT, summer plumage, about 1/2 (for winter plumage see p, 177)

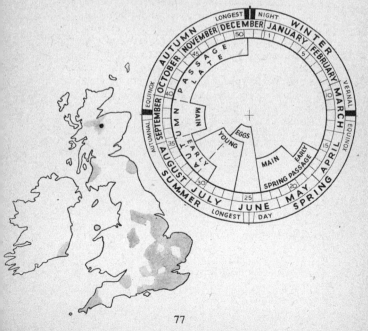

PURPLE SANDPIPER

Calidris maritima (BRÜNNICH) 1764.

RECOGNITION. Small. Length about 8 in. Larger than dunlin. Robust and portly. Bill brown-black, yellow at base, legs dull yellow. An active runner. White wing-bar noticeable in flight. Winter plumage (p. 177) dark, back dark-blackish ; head, neck and breast sooty-brown, throat and belly white. In summer rufous edgings to feathers. In winter most often in small flocks on rocky shores ; flocks perform evolutions in flight. Uses bill to pick rather than probe ; feeds on fish, insects, crustaceans, molluscs and plant-matter. Voice " wheat-whit " but often rises silently. Other notes on breeding-grounds. Very tame.

    DISTRIBUTION AND MOVEMENTS. Breeds round Polar Basin from Canadian Arctic, N. Europe, to Cape Chelyuskin. Another subspecies in Bering Sea. Extends as breeder to Iceland and Faeroes but not Britain, where passenger and winter visitor. Does *not* winter, as a whole, very far south ; not beyond U.S. in N. America, in Europe usually no further than Britain, France and Baltic, though sometimes to Mediterranean. Contrast this with other arctic breeders, *e.g.*, curlew-sandpiper. Main stream through Britain arrives Shetland and Orkney and there separates into western and eastern elements. Western element goes via Hebrides to Ireland where separates into a stream down west coast Ireland and streams down E. Ireland and W. Britain. Eastern element by usual route down east coast and along south coast. Keep to rocky parts of coast and if found inland probably storm-driven.

    TO READ. D. B. Keith (1938). *Observations on the purple sandpiper in North East Land.* Proceedings of the Zoological Society of London, vol. 108, series A, pp. 185-94.

PURPLE SANDPIPER, summer plumage, about 3/8 (for winter plumage see p. 177)

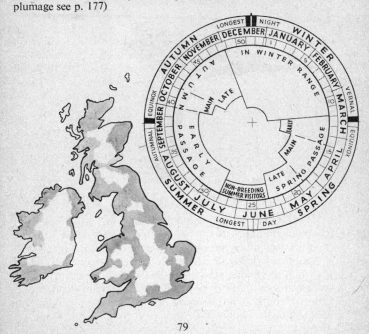

SANDERLING *Crocethia alba* (PALLAS) 1764.

SANDERLING, summer plumage, about 3/8

SANDERLING, winter plumage, about 3/8

RECOGNITION. Small. Length about 8 in. Slightly larger than dunlin. Plump. Black bill and legs. Very active runner. White wing-bar more prominent than in dunlin. In winter adult has upper-parts pale grey with faint dark markings, most of head and all under-parts white (phalaropes, which in winter might be confused, have dark patch on face and are slender, not plump), and dark front to wing. In summer quite different from dunlin with whole head, neck and breast light chestnut, and chestnut mottled with black on back. In flight flocks highly co-ordinated but do not do such complicated evolutions as those of dunlin. On ground flock runs like stream of hurried ants. Feeds by picking and probing on beaches and sandy flats ; eats crustaceans, molluscs and worms ; insects and seeds on breeding-grounds. Voice outside breeding-grounds " twick twick."

DISTRIBUTION. An arctic species and trans-equatorial migrant. Breeding-grounds have only been discovered in Canadian Arctic, N. Greenland, Spitsbergen and parts of Siberia. Not Iceland. Penetrates to southern S. America, S. Africa, E. Indies and Australasia in winter, but some winter well to north of equator as in Britain, where also passenger.

MOVEMENTS. Two main passages, of about equal density. Eastern element from Shetland and Orkney down normal east coast route, divides on reaching Lowlands, giving off branch continuing down east coast, and branch crossing overland to W. Lowlands, continuing down W. Britain and E. Ireland. Western element through outer Hebrides and Tiree to N. and W. Ireland.

TO READ. C. T. Dalgety, J. H. McNeile and M. J. Ingram (1931). *Notes on birds observed in Spitsbergen during the spring of* 1930. Ibis, series 13, vol. 1, pp. 243-55.

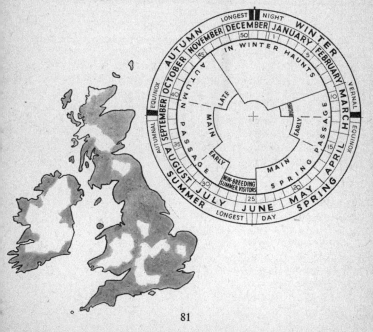

RUFF *Philomachus pugnax* (LINNAEUS) 1758.

RECOGNITION. Small. Length of ruff (male) about 11 in., of reeve (female) about 9 in. Heavier than common sandpiper. Bill black-brown, lighter at base. Legs very variable in colour, yellow, grey, green ; erect stance ; rapid strong flight with glides— flocks small and do not perform aerial evolutions ; narrow, not very clear, white wing-bar ; light areas on each side of dark central area of tail give impression of clear oval white patches. Young on autumn passage most often seen ; back has bold black-brown pattern, rich buff breast, throat and rest of underparts white. Summer reeve similar but greyer and tendency towards barring on breast. Sexes alike in plumage (but not size) in winter (p. 178) when colour tends towards fairly uniform grey. In summer ruffs assume the ruffs and ear-tufts, of a great variety of colour-schemes, which make identification a matter of no difficulty. Feeds by both probing and picking on insects, worms, crustaceans, molluscs and seeds. Usually silent, but note " tu-whit." Sometimes on estuaries but mostly inland by marshy shores and bogs.

DISTRIBUTION. Breeds from France and Central Europe north to the arctic mainland of Europe, and in central Russia and Siberia. Used to breed in Britain (see maps) but now extinct. Winters in and passes through countries between these and S. Africa, shores of Indian Ocean and E. Indies.

MOVEMENTS. In Britain main passage is down normal east coast route ; there is apparently no great use of the western routes, and birds found (rarely) on passage or in winter in West Country, Wales and Ireland are thought to have penetrated there cross-country by inland routes diverging from east coast routes. Certainly a fairly common visitor in autumn to inland sewage-farms in Midlands.

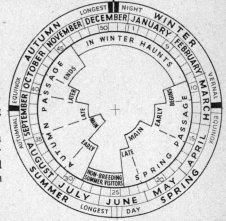

RUFF, summer plumage, about 3/10 (for winter plumage see p. 178)

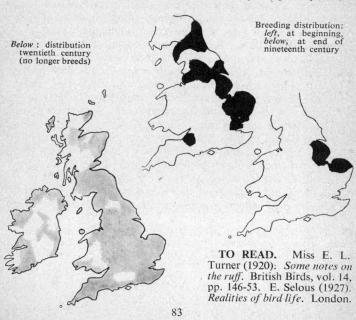

Below : distribution twentieth century (no longer breeds)

Breeding distribution: *left*, at beginning, *below*, at end of nineteenth century

TO READ. Miss E. L. Turner (1920): *Some notes on the ruff*. British Birds, vol. 14, pp. 146-53. E. Selous (1927). *Realities of bird life*. London.

COMMON SANDPIPER

Actitis hypoleucos (LINNAEUS) 1758.

RECOGNITION. Very small. Length just under 8 in. Bill dark brown, legs greenish; typical bobbing motion of body; very typical low flicking flight with short glides, wings appear curiously bent, well-defined wing-bar ; upper-parts brownish-grey flecked with dark in summer ; breast streaked ashy, rest of under-parts white in winter (p. 177). Seldom in flocks. Feeds by picking, not probing, on amphibians, spiders, molluscs, crustaceans, worms and insects. Shrill note " twee-wee-wee " outside breeding-season. Found in estuaries, but mostly inland by rocky shores and streams.

BREEDING. Solitary. Male has flight- and ground-displays. In flight ascends in fluttering spiral singing " titti-wee-wi " many times repeated, often in crescendo ; on ground does normal wader-type bowings and wing-liftings. Nests inland close to water, on banks, or in grass or heather, sometimes in woods, in hollows lined grass. Eggs 3-5, normally 4, length about 1½ in., greyish-buff with chestnut markings. Both sexes incubate for 3 weeks or more, and both manage young for about 4 weeks. Nestling buff, peppered with black on back, with brown line, under-parts mostly white. Young gets adult plumage in first season after that in which it is hatched.

DISTRIBUTION. Breeds from southern to arctic (mainland) Europe, and in Asia and has (most remarkably) nested on the Equator in Africa. Normally migrates to and through countries between its breeding-range and S. Africa, Indian Ocean, E. Indies and Australasia ; most birds at least leave Europe. In Britain summer visitor and passage migrant ; winter visitors are very rare.

MOVEMENTS. In Britain the west coast routes are more important than the east, contrary to the usual rule among waders. East coast route probably used mainly by birds that do not breed in Britain. Of the west coast routes, most used are those along N.W. England, Wales and the West Country, and along east coast Ireland. Inland routes on west side England also used extensively.

TO READ. G. C. S. Ingram (1945). *Common sandpipers on migration in South Glamorgan.* British Birds, vol. 38, pp. 169-72.

COMMON SANDPIPER, summer plumage, about 3/8 (for winter plumage see p. 177)

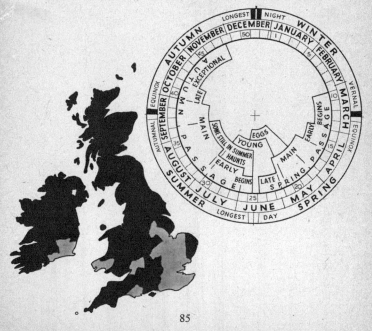

WOOD-SANDPIPER *Tringa glareola* (LINNAEUS) 1758.

RECOGNITION. Small. Length about 8 in. Dark and white in winter and summer ; more slender, lighter in colour and legs longer than green sandpiper. " Sandpiper-like " in all respects. Underside of wing light grey ; upper-parts appear mottled grey-brown in winter, under-parts more heavily marked than in green sandpiper with head, neck and breast streaked grey-brown (see p. 178) ; in summer back is conspicuously mottled and chequered with white markings and breast is streaked with brown ; white patch less bold than green sandpiper's (but still conspicuous) as confined to rump only, tail barred. Flight rapid. Feeds by picking and probing on worms, insects, spiders and molluscs. In Britain haunts inland marshes and creeks, singly or in small flocks. Voice away from breeding-grounds " chiff-chiff," which is best character to distinguish it from green sandpiper ; if rises silent look for position of feet which project beyond tail in wood- but not in green sandpiper.

DISTRIBUTION AND MOVEMENTS. Breeds in Europe from the arctic southwards to Holland, S. Baltic countries and N. Balkans ; and in Russian Asia. In autumn moves as far south as Australasia and S. Africa ; does not winter north of the Mediterranean or India. Has not bred in Britain for nearly a hundred years. Is a very occasional non-breeding summer visitor but is chiefly known as a passenger along the southern part of the normal east coast route, particularly between Lincs. and Kent.

WOOD-SANDPIPER, summer plumage, about 3/8 (for winter plumage see p. 178)

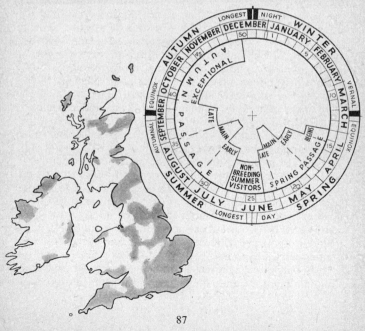

GREEN SANDPIPER *Tringa ochropus* (LINNAEUS)1758.

RECOGNITION. Small. Length about 9 in. Rump and most of tail conspicuously white. Is larger, stouter and darker than wood-sandpiper, and has shorter legs ; feet do not project beyond tail in flight. Underside of wing is blackish, which accentuates its " black-and-whiteness." Upper-parts appear black in winter, under-parts white with grey on breast (see p. 178) ; in summer white spotting on dark mantle finer than on wood-sandpiper. and breast less streaked. Shy. Flight strong, rather " tumbling," and in general habit " sandpiper-like." Feeds by picking and probing and even swimming and up-ending on insects, worms, crustaceans, spiders and molluscs. Flocks never large ; when flushed together birds tend to fly off as individuals. Voice " wit, wit," " kwee-weet-tweet " and variants ; parts of breeding song occasionally heard on passage.

BREEDING. Solitary. Male song-flight consists of circling followed by usual steep glide, uttering song " klu-ludle-lu-ludle-lu-ludle " and variants. Usual wader-type ground display, bowing with spread tail and arched wings. Also male and female play leap-frog. Nests in old marshy woods using old nests of other animals ; lined moss. Eggs 2-5, normally 4, length about 1½ in., olive-brown with a few spots. Female incubates about 3 weeks ; both pairs manage young for over a week after which male alone manages for unknown period. Nestling has bold pattern of pink and brown on back ; white underneath. Young practically attains adult plumage in first summer after that in which it is hatched. Flocks play social water-games in autumn, swimming and diving and splashing.

DISTRIBUTION. In Britain proved to breed in Lakes, 1917, and breeding behaviour noted Norfolk, Speyside and other places several years, though breeding not proved. Normally a passage migrant though some stay winter and quite a number of non-breeders stay summer. In Europe and Asia breeding distribution very like wood-sandpiper's but extends not so far into the Arctic, and further south. Does not migrate so far across equator ; in Africa not to south and in East not to Australasia.

MOVEMENTS. Main passage in Britain in autumn appears to be down north part of east coast route and elements in west counties derived from this by overland routes ; birds inland follow river-valleys and very regular at sewage farms. Reach Ireland in autumn but apparently do not return through it in spring.

GREEN SANDPIPER, summer plumage, about 1/3 (for winter plumage see p. 178)

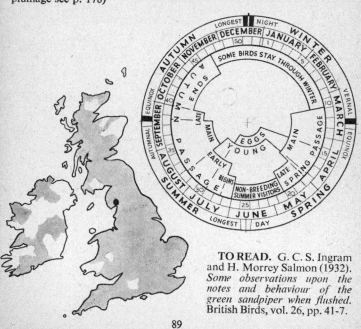

TO READ. G. C. S. Ingram and H. Morrey Salmon (1932). *Some observations upon the notes and behaviour of the green sandpiper when flushed.* British Birds, vol. 26, pp. 41-7.

REDSHANK *Tringa totanus* (LINNAEUS) 1758.

RECOGNITION. Small. Length about 11 in. Legs orange-red (yellow in young) ; bill orange at base ; broad white cres-cent on hind border of wing ; upper-parts brown and grey in winter (see p. 179) and marked with black in summer; white rump and on tail. Flight strong and fast, inclined to be " tumbl-ing," feet only project slightly behind tail. Feeds by picking and probing on insects, molluscs, crustaceans, worms, spiders, fish and amphibians, also plant-matter. Singly or in flocks. Shy. Voice " too," and " too-oo-oo " higher than greenshank. Other notes, especially in breeding-season.

BREEDING. Solitary. Song-flight of usual wader type, but may be performed by both sexes. Rises on trembling wings and glides in, singing " ta-weeo-ta-weeo-ta-weeo." Pursuits on ground of female by male, also usual wader-type bowing cere-mony. Nests in water-meadows, pasture-fields and on moors usually near water, in tufts ; nest lined grass. Eggs 3-5, usually 4, usually buff with brown spots, length about $1\frac{3}{4}$ in. Both sexes incubate for 3 to $3\frac{1}{2}$ weeks and both manage young for about 4 weeks. Nestling has pattern of brown and pinkish-buff on upper-parts, under-parts white. Young attains adult plumage in second summer after that in which it is hatched.

DISTRIBUTION. *Tringa totanus britannica* is the subspecies resident in Britain, widely distributed (see map) and increasing. Iceland redshank, *T. t. robusta* has been identified from measure-ments or by ringed birds as regular winter visitor. Continental redshank, *T. t. totanus*, is impossible to distinguish in the field, and only one specimen has been identified, but it seems likely that the great influx of redshanks which takes place in autumn in certain parts of both east and west coasts must be partly made up of continental elements.

MOVEMENTS. British redshanks show partial migration. Most simply disperse to feeding-grounds near breeding-grounds. A small proportion migrate, some from England and Scotland to Ireland, others to nearby continent. Passage of Iceland, prob-ably some continental, and the migrating element of British redshanks is by all normal routes along east and west coasts, and by overland routes along river valleys, often halting on water meadows and sewage farms.

TO READ. H. F. Witherby and N. F. Ticehurst (1940). *The continental redshank as a British bird.* British Birds, vol. 33, pp. 225-7. J. F. Thomas (1942). *Report on the redshank inquiry* 1939-40. British Birds, vol. 36, pp. 5-14, 22-34.

REDSHANK, summer plumage, about 1/4 (for winter plumage see p. 179)

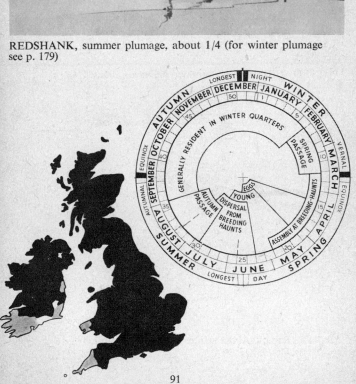

SPOTTED REDSHANK

Tringa erythropus (PALLAS) 1764.

SPOTTED REDSHANK, summer plumage, about 1/4

SPOTTED REDSHANK, winter plumage, about 1/4

RECOGNITION. Small-medium. Length about a foot. Legs very dark red ; bill dusky-red at base ; white spots but no marginal crescent on wing ; plumage (upper and under) very dark, spotted or streaked with white in summer (rump, of course, white as in all " shanks " described here) ; in winter more ashy-grey than redshank on upper-parts, white under-parts (see p. 179). Flight as redshank but feet and part of legs project beyond tail. Feeds by picking and probing on insects, molluscs, worms, crustaceans, fish and amphibians. Singly or in small parties. Shy. Voice outside breeding-season " chew-it " ; easy to distinguish from greenshank or redshank.

DISTRIBUTION AND MOVEMENTS. An arctic species, breeding from arctic Scandinavia to Siberia. Migrates in autumn to Mediterranean and Africa, and to southern Asia. In Britain strictly on passage, especially on southern England section of east coast route ; also a west coast element which crosses Lowlands from east to west, proceeds south to Cheshire, and apparently passes further south by inland routes. Small numbers regularly inland on passage up or down main river valleys and at reservoirs and sewage farms.

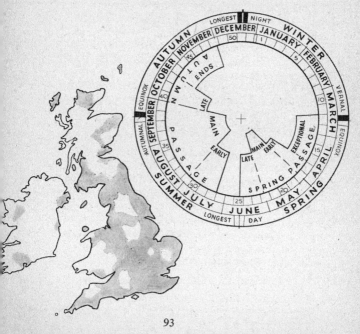

93

GREENSHANK *Tringa nebularia* (GUNNERUS) 1767.

RECOGNITION. Small-medium. Length about a foot. Greenish legs. Blue-slate, slightly up-curved bill. No white on wing. White rump, and on lower back and on tail. Flight strong and rapid, may twist but does not usually " tumble " as redshank ; in flight feet project beyond tail. Feeds by picking and probing on insects, crustaceans, worms, molluscs, amphibians and fish ; may chase fish by running in shallow water. Singly or in small parties. Shy. Voice away from breeding-ground " too-too-too," lower than redshank.

BREEDING. Solitary. Song-flight of usual wader type, most usually by male, but sometimes by female. Rises on trembling wings and glides down singing " ree-oo-too-oo, ree-oo-too-oo." Pursuit on ground of female by male, also usual wader-type bowing and wing-lifting ceremonies. Also male and female play leap-frog. Nests often as many as 4 miles from loch-side feeding-grounds on open moorland, often near boggy ground, or in very open type of Scots pine forest surviving in parts of Highlands ; in hollow or tussock lined heather and stems. Eggs 3-5, normally 4, buff with red-brown blobs and streaks, length about 2 in. Both sexes, but mostly female, incubate for $3\frac{1}{2}$ weeks and manage young for about 4 weeks. Nestlings striped on upper-parts warm buff and black, under-parts white. Young practically attains adult plumage in first year after that in which it is hatched.

DISTRIBUTION. Breeds in arctic and northern Europe and Russian Asia (to tree limit), but not far south of Baltic shores ; passes in autumn as far south as southern Australasia, India and Africa and does not normally winter north of the Mediterranean, Black Sea, India and China. Many Scandinavian birds pass through Britain. Very rarely winters in Britain.

MOVEMENTS. Passes in autumn along all usual routes. East coast route used from Shetland southwards, and west coast route from O. Hebrides southwards. Elements diverge westwards from east coast route to join west coast routes cross-country, and much general overland movement up and down main river valleys and via reservoirs and sewage farms. Most important west coast routes are those along west coast Ireland (which some Scottish breeders use) and west coasts England and Wales.

TO READ. Desmond and Caroline Nethersole-Thompson (1940) Sections on greenshank in *The handbook of British birds*, ed. H. F Witherby and others, London, vol. 4, pp. 336-8.

GREENSHANK, summer plumage, about 1/4 (for winter plumage see p. 179)

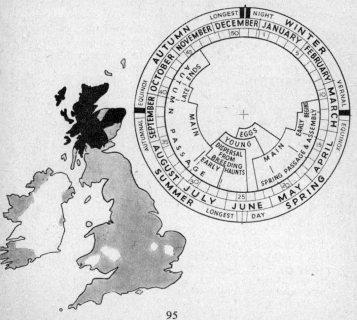

RINGED PLOVER *Charadrius hiaticula* (LINNAEUS) 1758.

RECOGNITION. Very small. Length 7 or 8 in. Robust. Conspicuous white collar and under-parts ; white wing-bar and no white band over head above black forehead-band distinguish from little ringed plover, as does larger size, yellowness of legs, and note. Black band round breast and *wide* dark band " through " eye distinguish from Kentish plover. Flight swift and low; flocks perform evolutions. Feeds rapidly, running along shore or mud with sudden stops to pick up (does not probe for) molluscs, insects, crustaceans and worms. Flocks medium-sized, cohesive. Fairly tame. Voice " tooli " ; other notes, especially on breeding-grounds.

BREEDING. Solitary. Display is low, moth-like flight in which birds flit and zig-zag about, singing a trilling, piping " pit-a-lee-o, pit-a-lee-o." Male also bows and scrapes before female, rapidly marks time with feet, or chases her on ground. Nests on shores, marshes, heaths, shingle-banks, in hollow ; nest material varies with environment from nothing to grass-stems. Eggs 3-5, usually 4, greyish with dark spots, length up to 1½ in. Both sexes incubate eggs for about 3½ weeks and manage young for about the same period, and normally start second brood as soon as young are fledged. Nestling grey-buff speckled, spotted and striped with black-brown on upper-parts ; under-parts white. Young are usually indistinguishable from adults in first summer after that in which they are hatched.

DISTRIBUTION. Common ringed plover, *C. h. hiaticula*, breeds in chain Baffin Island—S. Greenland—Iceland—Faeroes —Britain—non-arctic Scandinavia and shores of Baltic—France —Spain and Portugal—north shores Mediterranean east to Italy. Arctic ringed plover, *C. h. tundrae*, breeds in European and Siberian Arctic. Common ringed plover migrates no further than Europe, N. and W. Africa and Canaries, but arctic sub-species reaches S. Africa. In Britain common race breeds widely inland and is also passage migrant and winter visitor ; arctic race is passenger and winter visitor.

MOVEMENTS. Both races use usual E. and W. coastal routes with a good deal of overland " leakage " from E. route to W. at all levels from Highlands to S. England. Some Scottish and N. English breeders certainly pass to, and through, Ireland.

TO READ. T. L. Smith (1921). *A ringed plover's nests.* British Birds, vol. 15, pp. 26-32. G. Marples (1931). *Experimental studies of the ringed plover.* British Birds, vol. 25, pp. 34-44.

RINGED PLOVER, about 2/5 (see also p. 180)

LITTLE RINGED PLOVER

Charadrius dubius SCOPOLI 1786.

RECOGNITION. Very small. Length about 6 in. Robust. Conspicuous white collar and under-parts ; no white wing-bar, and narrow white band over head above black forehead-band distinguish from common ringed plover, as does small size, dull flesh colour of legs, and note. Black band round breast and wide dark band " through " eye distinguish from Kentish plover. Flight like ringed plover. Feeds by running and picking on insects, spiders, molluscs and worms. Small flocks outside breeding-season. Voice " teu " or " pee-o " higher pitched than ringed plover ; other notes on breeding-grounds.

BREEDING. Solitary. Display very similar to ringed plover's with moth-like flight and marking time by male. Song a trilling " pee-u-pee-u-pee-u." Nests on shores and shingle-banks, usually inland ; hollow, lined stems, sometimes unlined. Eggs 3-5, normally 4, length up to $1\frac{1}{4}$ in., green-buff with small spots. Both sexes incubate about $3\frac{1}{2}$ weeks and tend young for 3 weeks or more ; sometimes have second brood. Nestling like ringed plover's but redder. Young are usually indistinguishable from adults in first summer after that in which they are hatched.

DISTRIBUTIONS AND MOVEMENTS. In Britain very rare passage migrant, practically unknown outside S.E. England, and very rare there. Pair reared brood Tring Reservoirs, Herts., in 1938. In 1944 two pairs bred at Tring Reservoirs and another pair reared young in a gravel-pit near Ashford, Middlesex. *Charadrius dubius curonicus*, the subspecies of Europe and Northern Asia, normally breeds from N. Europe and Siberia (just into Arctic) south to N. Africa and Persia, and in intermediate countries. In autumn migrates beyond (but not far beyond) Equator in Africa and Asia. Britain seems to be the only part of temperate Europe outside its *normal* range.

TO READ. R. C. B. Ledlie and E. G. Pedler (1938). *Nesting of the little ringed plover in Hertfordshire.* British Birds, vol. 32, pp. 90-102. M. D. England, E. O. Höhn, E. G. Pedler and B. W. Tucker (1944). *The breeding of the little ringed plover in England in 1944.* British Birds, vol. 38, pp. 102-111.

LITTLE RINGED PLOVER, about 1/2 (see also p. 180)

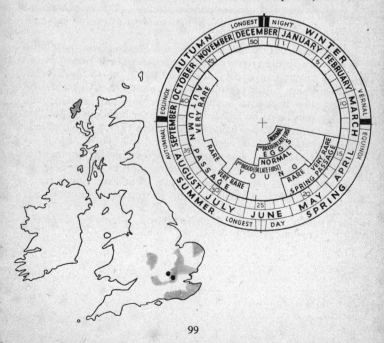

KENTISH PLOVER
Leucopolius alexandrinus (LINNAEUS) 1758.

RECOGNITION. Very small. Length about 6 in. Robust. Conspicuous white collar and under-parts ; not very prominent white wing-bar. Lead-grey legs ; dark patches on sides of breast instead of continuous dark band round breast ; and *narrow* dark band " through " eye distinguish it from the two ringed plovers. Flight like ringed plovers. Feeds by running and picking on insects, molluscs, spiders, worms and crustaceans. Small flocks outside breeding-season. Voice " pit-pit-pit," and " peu-i " ; other notes on breeding-grounds ; less shrill than ringed plovers.

BREEDING. Solitary. Display appears to be like ringed plover's with moth-flight. Song develops " pit-pit-pit " into purring trill. Nests on shores and shingle-banks, hollow with no lining or stems. Eggs 2-5, normally 3, length usually over $1\frac{1}{4}$ in., buff with black streaks. Both sexes incubate about $3\frac{1}{2}$ weeks and tend young for unknown period (? 3 or 4 weeks) ; sometimes have second brood. Nestling lighter colour on back than ringed plovers but general pattern similar. Young practically indistinguishable from adults in first summer after that in which they are hatched.

DISTRIBUTION. *Leucopolius a. alexandrinus* has very similar distribution to *curonicus* subspecies of little ringed plover (p. 98) except that it does not breed so far north, and breeds further south, to the central Atlantic Islands, N. Africa and N. India. Britain, again, seems to be the only part of temperate Europe outside its *normal* range, except for breeding population in Kent which has not bred regularly since 1931, and which may now be extinct.

MOVEMENTS. European birds winter as far south as S. Africa. In Britain rare as a passage migrant in *spring* along the English part of the east coast route, even rarer same region autumn, and exceptionally rare anywhere else, or at any other time.

TO READ. Norman F. Ticehurst (1909). *A history of the birds of Kent.* London, Witherby & Co., pp. 420-6.

KENTISH PLOVER, about 1/2 (see also p. 180)

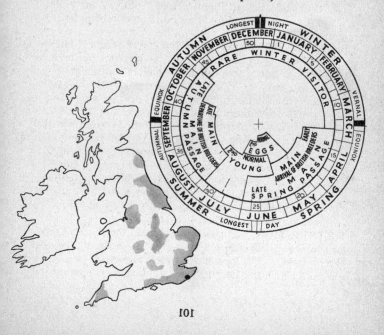

GOLDEN PLOVER *Pluvialis apricaria* (LINNAEUS) 1758.

RECOGNITION. Small. Length about 11 in. No white collar (compare ringed plovers). Larger than dotterel. Upper-parts spangled dark and light; under-parts light in winter, mostly dark in summer. Legs grey. Distinguished from grey plover by having upper-parts spangled black and gold, by having patch of *white* feathers in axilla (arm-pit) under wing, and by having a more slender bill. Also has dark rump and tail and no wing-bar. In winter golden plovers have under-parts whitish with some dark mottlings, and it is impossible to distinguish the northern and southern subspecies. In summer, however, the northern subspecies has face, cheeks, and under-parts black, separated from upper-parts by a broad white band; while the southern subspecies (the one which breeds in Britain) has a dusky face, a mottled throat, black on breast and belly flecked with light feathers and not separated from upper-parts by a pure white band. Flight fast and steady, often travels at some height. Flocks outside breeding-season, often large, perform evolutions. Feeds by running and picking on insects, molluscs, worms, spiders and seeds. In winter often with lapwings; flocks separate in flight. Note " t'loo-i " or " taludl," very liquid, carries far; many other notes especially on breeding-grounds.

BREEDING. Solitary. Male has " moth-flight " but high in air, not low as in ringed plovers, ending in dive, and also has darting, erratic display-flight. Song in moth-flight " tirr-pee-you, tirr-pee-you "; also has rippling " taludl-taludl-taludl " on ground and in flight. Males also have tendency to " leks " or display-gatherings of their own sex; at leks and with females do usual wader-type wing-lifting, bowing, scraping, leap-frogging and chasing. Nests inland on moorland or tundra; nest in scrape, lined stalks. Eggs 3-4, normally 4, length about 2 in., buff blotched with dark brown. Both sexes incubate for 4 weeks and tend young for 4 weeks. Nestling has pattern of yellow-white and black; under-parts grey-white. Young cannot be distinguished from adults in the first breeding-season after that in which they are hatched.

DISTRIBUTION. *Pluvialis a. apricaria*, the southern golden plover, breeds in Britain, Holland and round the shores of the southern Baltic. The northern golden plover, *P. a. altifrons*, breeds in Iceland, the Faeroes and arctic Europe, south to the

continued on p. 104

SOUTHERN GOLDEN PLOVER, summer plumage, about 2/7 (for winter plumage see p. 181)

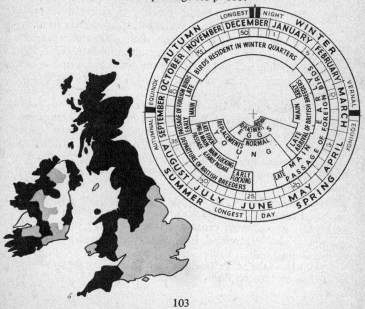

northern Baltic, and east into Siberia. As the races cannot be distinguished out of breeding-plumage we do not know whether both races travel as far as N. Africa, Arabia and N. India which appear to be the southward limits of the species in winter. In Britain the northern race is a regular passenger and winter visitor. As the former it has been identified in breeding dress, or in the first or last signs of it ; as the latter from birds marked in Iceland.

MOVEMENTS. All normal coastal routes used, and many inland. East coast route much used in N. Scotland, but elements filter away overland to join west coast routes (many going to Ireland) so that relatively few pass through S.E. England.

TO READ. Desmond Nethersole-Thompson (1940). Sections on golden plover in *The handbook of British birds*, ed. H. F. Witherby and others, London, vol. 4, pp. 365-6.

W440-1

GREY PLOVER *Squatarola squatarola* (LINNAEUS) 1758.

RECOGNITION. Small. Length about 11 in. Like golden plover but upper-parts spangled black and grey (some yellow on young). Stouter bill than golden plover ; in winter upper-parts less spangled, more uniform. Patch of black feathers in axilla (arm-pit) under wing. Has whitish rump, tail and wing-bar. Flight fast and steady. Flocks on passage, usually small. Shy. Feeds by running and picking on worms, molluscs, crustaceans, insects and seeds. Note very like golden plover's but higher and less liquid.

DISTRIBUTION. An arctic breeder, restricted to some islands and coasts of the Polar Basin, in all three continents. Spreads over most of the world on passage and in winter, reaching S. Africa, southern S. America and Australasia. In Britain mainly a passage migrant, but quite a number winter, and a few non-breeders summer ; more strictly a coastal species than golden plover.

MOVEMENTS. Chief immigration in autumn appears to be in N.E. Scotland ; birds continue down east coast route to Lowlands, where some cross overland to west ; thence form main passages—W. Ireland, E. Ireland, W. England and Wales, E. and S. England.

TO READ. Miss M. D. Haviland (1915). *Notes on the grey plover on the Yenesei.* British Birds, vol. 9, pp. 162-6.

GREY PLOVER, summer plumage, about 2/7 (for winter plumage see p. 181)

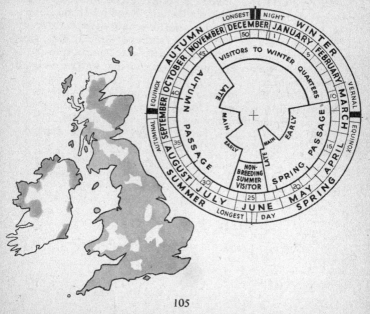

DOTTEREL *Eudromias morinellus* (LINNAEUS) 1758.

RECOGNITION. Small. Length about 9 in. Smaller than golden and grey plovers. Broad white eye-stripes meeting at back of head ; dark breast separated from chestnut belly by white band. In winter pattern much duller and markedly less contrast. Legs dull yellow. Flight fast and steady. Flocks small. Very tame. Feeds by running and picking on insects, spiders, molluscs, worms and seeds. Piping note outside breeding-grounds " wit-e-wee " ; other notes in breeding-season.

BREEDING. Solitary. Inverted sex-rôles. Most display by female, includes display-flight with zig-zags and glides, wing-lifting, bowing and scraping, leap-frogging, chasing. Nest on stony or mossy alpine or sub-alpine zones of high hills in Britain (or on tundra in arctic). Scrape lined moss and grass. Eggs 2-4, normally 3, length up to $1\frac{3}{4}$ in., buff with black-brown blotches. Male practically alone incubates 3 to $3\frac{1}{2}$ weeks, and tends young 4 to $4\frac{1}{2}$ weeks. Nestling has upper-parts with pattern of white, black and buff ; under-parts grey-white. Young cannot usually be distinguished from adults in the first breeding-season after that in which they are hatched.

DISTRIBUTION. Breeds in arctic Europe and Asia, otherwise only on high mountains in Britain, Scandinavia and Europe north of the Danube, and in north central Asia. Moves in winter as far south as N. Africa and shores of Arabian Sea. Has been getting rarer in Britain ; used to breed fairly recently in Lowlands. Outside breeding range mainly known as rare spring passenger.

MOVEMENTS. In Britain much more common in *spring* than on autumn passage. Does not use orthodox coastal routes but filters through inland routes mostly on east side Britain.

TO READ. G. G. Blackwood (1920). *Notes on the breeding-habits of the dotterel* (Eudromias morinellus) *in Scotland.* Scottish Naturalist for 1920, pp. 185-94. E. Blezard (1926). *Breeding of the dotterel on the Pennines in* 1925. British Birds, vol. 20, pp. 17-19. Desmond and Caroline Nethersole-Thompson (1940). Sections on dotterel in *The handbook of British birds*, ed. H. F. Witherby and others, London, vol. 4, pp. 384-6.

DOTTEREL, summer plumage, about 1/3

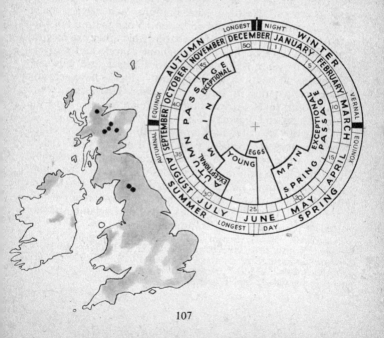

LAPWING *Vanellus vanellus* (LINNAEUS) 1758.

RECOGNITION. Small-medium. Length about a foot. Upperparts metallic green with white rump and white on head ; underparts white with black on breast and reddish under tail ; conspicuous crest ; short black bill ; brown legs. In flight wings appear rounded ; flight tumbling but fairly fast. Flocks often very large and perform evolutions which, compared with those of other waders, are in " slow-motion." Rather shy. Feeds by running and picking on insects, molluscs, worms, spiders, crustaceans and seeds. Call " pee-wit," unmistakable, with elaborations on breeding-grounds.

BREEDING. Semi-social, but sometimes quite solitary. Male has tumbling and plunging display-flight during which appears to turn somersaults in air ; in this flight has vocal song " whey-willuch-coowhee, willuch-willuch-coowhee " which is followed by wing-humming. Also bows and scrapes and wing-lifts on ground; and occasionally plays leap-frog. Nests on farmland and moors in scrape lined with stems. Eggs 3-5, normally 4, buff spotted with black, length usually just under 2 in. Both sexes incubate about 4 weeks ; female tends young about $4\frac{1}{2}$ weeks. Nestling, back buff-grey and black ; underparts white with a black band on breast. Young attain full adult plumage in second summer after that in which they are hatched.

DISTRIBUTION. Breeds throughout Europe and west half of Asiatic Russia. Extends north to Faeroes and European arctic mainland, south to Mediterranean. Flocks have occasionally crossed Atlantic in autumn or winter, but normal winter range is south to N. Africa, shores Arabian Sea, N. India and Burma, China and Japan.

MOVEMENTS. Britain's large breeding-population is generally migratory in northern parts ; in England shows partial migration, some resident and others summer visitors. Summer visitors that leave Britain in autumn are " replaced " by continental winter visitors. A great passage also along normal coastal and some inland routes. Scottish breeders move largely by west routes to S.W. Ireland, S.W. Wales and S.W. England, and most east coast passengers are of continental origin.

TO READ. R. H. Brown (1926). *Some breeding-habits of the lapwing.* British Birds, vol. 20, pp. 162-8. H. F. Witherby (1928). *A transatlantic passage of lapwings.* British Birds, vol. 22, pp. 6-13. E. M. Nicholson (1938-9). *Report on the lapwing habitat inquiry,* 1937. British Birds, vol. 32, pp. 170-91, 207-29, 255-9.

LAPWING, summer plumage, about 2/9

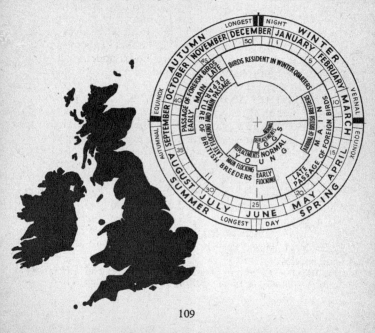

BLACK-WINGED STILT

Himantopus himantopus (LINNAEUS) 1758.

RECOGNITION. Small-medium. Length with bill but without legs about 15 in. Bill nearly 3 in., black and straight. White plumage with black mantle and wings ; summer male has black on head. Immensely long pink legs project about 7 in., or nearly half length of body, beyond tail in flight. Flight straight with rapid beats, legs act as rudder. Has been seen in flight to bring one leg forward to scratch head. Small flocks as a rule. Adapted for wading in deepish water, and normally feeds in water above leg-joint by picking animals from or near the surface. On dry land has to bend its legs to reach food with its bill. Eats insects, molluscs, worms and amphibians. Voice " kiweuk-kiweuk," or " kik-kik-kik " ; other variants on breeding-grounds.

BREEDING. Social. Male displays by dancing, to which female answers by bowing. Male holds body vertical, *i.e.*, " stands up," and waves wings forward slowly as if clapping hands, changing from one foot to another ; like a man in the cold stamping and beating his arms. Colonies on or near shallow lagoons and tanks, or flooded country or marsh, nests in tussocks or on ground, lined reeds. Eggs 3-5, normally 3, stone-colour with black spots, length about 1¾ in. Both sexes incubate eggs for about 3½ weeks and tend young until it flies in about 4½ weeks. Nestling light buff with black-brown lines, under-parts white. Male attains adult plumage in second, female in third summer after that in which they are hatched.

DISTRIBUTION AND MOVEMENTS. *H. h. himantopus*, the race found in Britain, breeds in *southern* Europe and Asia, south to South Africa and Ceylon. The stilts breeding in the temperate parts of this wide range migrate to the tropics in the winter. In western Europe normally breeds only in the Iberian Peninsula and the south of France, but from time to time minor irruptions take place into regions further north, and stilts have recently bred in the Netherlands. In 1945 an abnormal number of stilts were seen in England and a small colony (3 nests, 9 eggs laid, 4 young hatched, 3 young flew) bred on Nottingham sewage farm. Otherwise has been a rare wanderer, occasionally seen in Norfolk and very rarely anywhere else. Normally an inland species.

TO READ. J. Staton (1945). *The breeding of black-winged stilts in Nottinghamshire in 1945.* British Birds, vol. 38, pp. 322-8.

BLACK-WINGED STILT, about 1/5

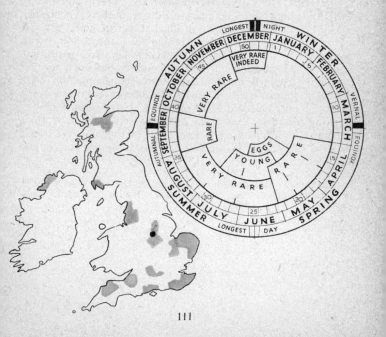

AVOCET *Recurvirostra avosetta* (LINNAEUS) 1758.

RECOGNITION. Small-medium. Length about 17 in. with bill. White plumage with bold, black bands on crown and back of neck, back and wings. Long upcurved black bill over 3 in. long. Very long blue-grey legs. Flight straight and steady with rapid beats, legs trail beyond tail. Feeds by walking, wading or swimming, swinging bill from side to side or " ducking " for insects, crustaceans and worms. Small flocks as a rule ; fairly tame. Voice a mellow " kluit " ; other notes on breeding-grounds.

BREEDING. Social. Remarkable absence of courtship display except such as is directly concerned with act of mating ; some curious and complicated social ceremonies. Colonies on flat ground near lagoons ; nest a hollow, sometimes lined. Eggs 3-5, usually 4, about 2 in. long, stone-buff with black spots. Both sexes incubate eggs about $3\frac{1}{2}$ weeks and tend young about 6 weeks. Nestling grey-buff with dark brown lines and mottling, under-parts creamy white. Young practically attains adult plumage in first season after that in which it is hatched.

DISTRIBUTION AND MOVEMENTS. Breeds at mouth of Baltic and along North Sea coast of Europe, in Iberian Peninsula, in S. of France, Balkans, shores of Black, Caspian, and Aral Seas ; east to China, south to shores Arabian Sea ; throughout Africa from north to south. Northern elements migrate to Africa and southern Asia, and some, from Baltic and N. Sea coast regions, pass fairly regularly through coastal areas England from Wash to Southampton Water. Elsewhere in Britain very rare indeed ; in Ireland only recorded about 20 times apart from astonishing breeding record in 1938 when 2 pairs nested in a place which remains a well-kept secret. Last bred in England just over a hundred years ago ; before that had large colonies in most east and south-east counties.

TO READ. W. E. Glegg (1925). *On the nesting of the avocet in the Camargue.* British Birds, vol. 19, pp. 82-7. J. S. Huxley (1925). *The absence of " courtship " in the avocet.* British Birds, vol. 19, pp. 88-94.

AVOCET, about 1/5

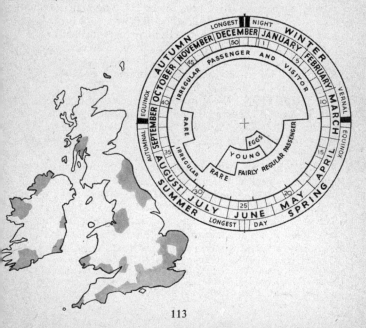

OYSTERCATCHER
Haematopus ostralegus (LINNAEUS) 1758.

RECOGNITION. Medium. Length about 17 in. Upper-parts glossy black except for white wing-bar and rump ; under-parts white. Long orange bill. Pink legs. Flies straight and low with fast rather short beats. Flocks outside breeding-season, often large. Fairly tame. Feeds largely on mussels and limpets, opens or dislodges them with special technique. Can open oysters. Also feeds by probing and picking. Besides molluscs eats crustaceans, worms, insects, echinoderms and even young birds and eggs. Voice noisy. " Kleep, kleep," or " quick, quick " ; other notes on breeding-grounds.

BREEDING. Solitary. Piping-parties seem to take place of most normal courtship display ; at these from one to a dozen, but usually 2 to 4 birds run in curves with bills pointed down uttering trilling " kewick, kewick, kwick, kwick, kwick, kwirrrrr . . ." Male also has butterfly-like silent display-flight. In Britain breeds inland up moorland rivers, as a normal thing in Highlands, and increasingly in recent years in Lowlands, N. England and W. Ireland. Nest by shore, on sand, grass or pebbles; often in dry river-beds inland. Lining material absent or scanty. Eggs 2-5, usually 3, stone-buff with dark brown spots and blobs, length about 2¼ in. Both parents incubate eggs 3½ to 4 weeks and manage young for about 5 weeks. Nestling black with buff stripes and speckling, mostly white under-parts. Young does not usually acquire full plumage until the second summer after that in which it is hatched.

DISTRIBUTION. The European subspecies of oystercatchers breed in Iceland, Faeroes, Britain and all along W. European coast from Arctic to S. Portugal; also along north shore Mediterranean and into Black Sea. Move in winter to and beyond equatorial Africa.

MOVEMENTS. Most British breeders, but not all, migrate a moderate distance. Main routes used are normal east and west coast routes. Highland birds and others from outside Britain take outer west route to N. and then W. Ireland. Another west route down W. England and Wales coast, but not many down E. Ireland coast. Many birds from outside Britain pass along or spend winter on east and south coast routes.

TO READ. E. J. M. Buxton (1939). *The breeding of the oyster-catcher.* British Birds, vol. 33, pp. 184-93. K. Williamson (1943). *The behaviour pattern of the western oyster-catcher . . . in defence of nests and young.* Ibis, vol. 85, pp. 486-90.

OYSTERCATCHER, summer plumage, about 1/5

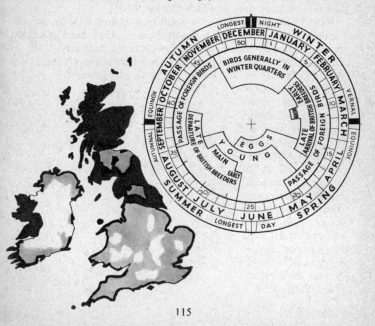

STONE-CURLEW *Burhinus oedicnemus* (LINNAEUS) 1758.

RECOGNITION. Medium. Length about 16 in. Large yellow eye. Streaked brown plumage. Flies straight and fast with fairly slow, steady wing-beats, and exhibits a conspicuous and unmistakable pattern of white and black on wings in flight. Feeds in small or medium-sized flocks (even in breeding-season), mostly by night, often "flighting" to feeding-grounds, on molluscs, worms, insects, small rodents, young birds and amphibians. Very shy. By day hides by crouching close to ground, motionless; cryptic pattern of plumage conceals. Runs extremely fast. Voice "coo-ee," other notes in breeding-season.

BREEDING. Solitary, though parents off-duty may flock and feed socially. Display on ground, with bowing, skipping, dancing and even rolling over. Breeds in England on open downland, practically restricted to the chalk and the breck. No real nest; eggs 2 or 3, usually 2, length about 2 in., stone-colour spotted dark brown. Both sexes incubate eggs $3\frac{1}{2}$ to 4 weeks and manage young for 6 weeks; may then, sometimes, produce second laying. Nestling sandy-buff with black lines, under-parts light buff. Young probably attains adult plumage in first season after that in which it is hatched.

DISTRIBUTION. Breeds north to S. Baltic, west to Britain, south to N. Africa and South Asia. Has been grouped into several subspecies. Northern elements migrate as far as Equator, including birds from Britain, where generally a summer visitor (a few winter in Devon, Cornwall and Dorset).

MOVEMENTS.
In Britain reach breeding - haunts apparently by direct overland routes, and thus seen on passage in southern counties in places (*e.g.*, estuaries and moors) where does not breed. Now only a vagrant in N. England, where used to breed, and extremely rare in Scotland and Ireland.

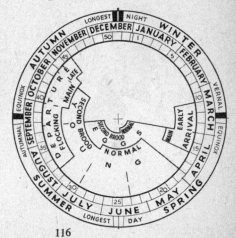

STONE-CURLEW, about 1/5

Above : breeding distribution in middle of nineteenth century ; compare breeding distribution twentieth century (left).

TO READ. E. Selous (1901). *Bird watching*. London. G. Bird (1933): *Some habits of the stone-curlew*. British Birds, vol. 27, pp. 114-6.

GREAT BUSTARD *Otis tarda* (LINNAEUS) 1758.

RECOGNITION. Immense. Length male about 3½ ft., weight may be as much as 45 lb. (heaviest flying bird) ; length female about 2½ ft. Essential field characters are sandy upper-parts barred with black ; heavy body ; much white on wing in flight. Flies straight and very fast with slow, steady wing-beats. Grazes in small or medium-sized flocks in very open country on cultivated and wild crops, grass and leaves—main diet vegetable, but also eats small mammals, birds, reptiles and amphibians, and molluscs, worms, insects and spiders. Exceptionally wary and shy. Normally walks, but can run fast. Voice a grunt, or " kang."

DISTRIBUTION AND MOVEMENTS. Breeding distribution now very much restricted, formerly wide. Today breeds in four main areas ; a " pocket " in south-west of Iberian Peninsula extending across Straits of Gibraltar into neighbouring parts of N. Africa ; another in E. Germany and Poland ; another from Hungary, south into Balkans and east into Rumania and Ukraine, and through Kirghiz Steppes into south-western Asiatic Russia ; another in Asia Minor and neighbouring countries. In eastern Asia a different subspecies. Used to breed in N.W. Europe and England ; last indigenous birds died in Norfolk a hundred years ago (1845). Now a very rare vagrant in Britain. Species generally held to be resident and sedentary but disperses from breeding-grounds in autumn and young birds tend to wander.

TO READ. H. Stevenson and Thos. Southwell (1870) *Birds of Norfolk*, London, vol. 2.

TO SEE. The late Horst Siewert's film of the display of the great bustard.

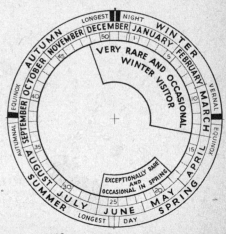

GREAT BUSTARD male, summer plumage, about 1/13

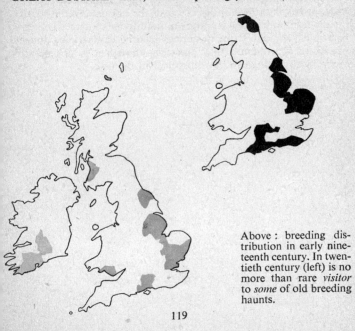

Above : breeding distribution in early nineteenth century. In twentieth century (left) is no more than rare *visitor* to *some* of old breeding haunts.

LITTLE BUSTARD _Otis tetrax_ LINNAEUS 1758.

RECOGNITION. Medium. Length about 17 in. Sandy mantle and white under-parts. Males in summer have pattern of bluish, white and black on head and neck. Does not fly straight, rises with rattle and flies fast with much quicker wing-beats than great bustard, showing much white on wing and, in fact, a generally white appearance in the air. Grazes in medium to large flocks in open country on cultivated crops, especially roots and corn, and on clover and grass ; also eats insects, worms, molluscs, amphibians and small mammals. Very wary and shy. Can run fast. Voice " dog."

DISTRIBUTION AND MOVEMENTS. Has a similar grouping to that of great bustard, but main " pockets " now held to constitute two separate subspecies. Western race, _O. t. tetrax_, breeds in France, Iberian Peninsula and Atlas mountain area. Eastern race, _O. t. orientalis_, breeds in Danube basin countries, Balkans, Ukraine through Kirghiz Steppes into south-west Asiatic Russia, and has a separate pocket south of Asia Minor in Syria and Palestine. Is migratory, unlike great bustard ; northern elements of both races moving in autumn beyond (but not far beyond) the southern edge of the normal breeding-range. In Britain both races are known, mainly as autumn wanderers. Curiously enough from specimens secured eastern race appears to be more common than western—though it is not possible reliably to distinguish the subspecies in the field.

LITTLE BUSTARD, male, summer plumage, about 1/6

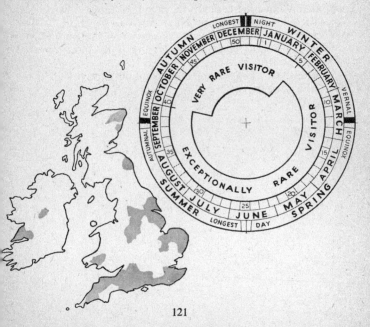

CRANE *Grus grus* (LINNAEUS) 1758.

RECOGNITION. Very large. Total length about 3 ft. 9 in., of which long neck takes up 1 ft. 9 in. and is held straight out in flight. Body uniformly grey. Bill relatively short. Legs long, trail beyond tail in flight. Secondary feathers of wing form what looks like festooned tail when wings are folded. Red patch on back of head. Fast, stately straight flight with steady, slow wing-beats. Flocks fly in V or V-arm formation uttering loud clanging calls ; small or medium-sized. Walks in stately fashion with body held half-upright and feeds by picking and probing on insects, molluscs, worms, amphibians, reptiles, small birds and mammals, and a considerable amount of plant matter, including seeds, roots and leaves, especially cultivated grains. Very wary and shy.

DISTRIBUTION AND MOVEMENTS. Breeds in wet fens and bogs. Last bred in Britain (Fen country) about 350 years ago. Now breeds in countries round Baltic and in European Russia with relict groups in Spain, Balkans and Asia Minor. A different subspecies in southern Asiatic Russia. Used to have a much wider distribution in Europe but draining of fens and cultivation have increasingly restricted its range. Migrates to N. Africa, in places (*e.g.*, up Nile) nearly to Equator. Used to winter in Britain until 100 years ago but now winters no further north than South Iberia and Italy, and is no more than rare wanderer to Britain today.

WARNING. Cranes are often kept in captivity in Britain and birds seen may prove to be " escapes."

CRANE, about 1/13

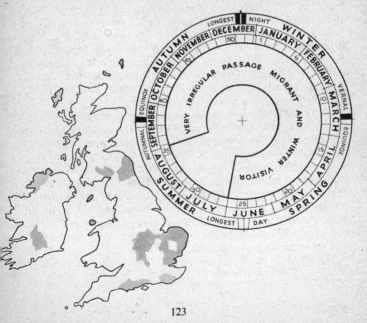

BLACK TERN *Chlidonias niger* (LINNAEUS) 1758.

RECOGNITION. Small. Length about 9 in. In summer uniform slate-grey and black except for white under tail. In winter black cap with white forehead ; under-parts white ; back and wings grey—grey extends down as patch on under-parts in front of base of wing. Bill black ; legs and feet red-brown, but look black. Flight not quite so " light " as that of most other British terns. Feeds by dropping to surface of water, or hovering above surface (very rarely diving), or hawking, on insects, spiders, leeches, fish and amphibians. Outside breeding-season individual or in small flocks. Voice " kik, kik."

BREEDING. Social. Display-flights. Colonies in marshes or flooded areas, nests of reeds, etc., often floating. Eggs 2 to 4, usually 3, about 1½ in. long, brown or green with blackish blotches. Both sexes incubate eggs 2 weeks or more, and manage young about 4 weeks. Nestling buff with black lines, under-parts grey. Young practically attains adult plumage in first season after that in which it is hatched.

DISTRIBUTION. Practically extinct as a breeding species in Britain a hundred years ago ; very last bred 1885. Used to breed in Yorkshire, the Fens, Broads and Romney Marsh. Remarkable recolonisation 1941, Pett Level, Sussex, where 8 nests found : bred also 1942 and possibly 1943. In Europe breeds from Spain to S. shore Baltic, and into Asia Minor and W. Russian Asia. A different subspecies in America. In autumn migrates through Africa to some distance beyond Equator ; some migrants pass through Britain, chiefly in area Wash to Thames-mouth and along Channel coast.

MOVEMENTS. Passage routes in Britain appear to consist of normal east coastal route Wash—Thamesmouth—Kent—Channel coast; and several subsidiary but quite important inland routes, using chains of inland lakes, reservoirs and sewage farms, which *appear* to be, in autumn, Forth-Clyde (small numbers), Tweed-Solway, Humber-Mersey, S. Lancs.-Cheshire Plain-Severn, Humber-Trent-Avon, up Nene and Ouse-down Thames. Birds that have come up Nene and Ouse, or down Severn and Avon, may cross to Thames and proceed down it; some from Severn appear to cross Somerset. Very rare in Ireland but some passage along inland lakes.

TO READ. R. B. Sibson (1939). *The black tern in the lower Thames.* British Birds, vol. 32, pp. 304-5. R. Cooke (1946). *Black terns breeding in Sussex.* British Birds, vol. 39, pp. 71-2.

BLACK TERN, summer plumage, about 3/10

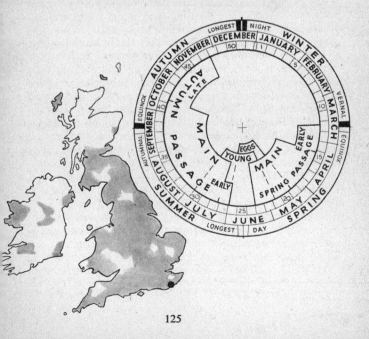

SANDWICH TERN *Sterna sandvicensis* LATHAM 1787.

RECOGNITION. Medium. Length about 16 in. Larger than other common British terns, and flight more gull-like. Tail not so forked ; wings very long and narrow ; bill black with yellow tips. Legs comparatively long, black ; feet black with yellow soles. Feathers on back of head long and can be raised as crest. In winter (p. 182), loses more of its black cap than other British terns. Flight more like gull's than other common terns. Dives direct from a considerable height for fish, of which mostly eats sand-eels. Also takes worms and molluscs. Social at all times. Usual call " kirrick " ; other notes on breeding-grounds.

BREEDING. Social. Display by both sexes. Main display is fish-flight; bird with fish is pursued and overtaken by another; motions may be gone through without a fish. Also swiftly glide from height. On ground parade and bow and scrape and scissor bills. Colonies on low rock, sand or gravel, usually by sea; nests a scrape lined grass. Eggs 1 to 3, normally 2, buff with black-brown spots, length about 2 in. Both sexes incubate eggs about 3 weeks and manage young for a week or fortnight after which young colony are " pooled." Young fly about 5 weeks after hatching. Nestling has " hairy " appearance; pattern of buff mottled black; white under-parts. Young attains adult plumage in second summer after that in which it is hatched.

DISTRIBUTION. Breeds in four groups : S. Baltic—mainland shores N. Sea—Britain—Brittany; Central Mediterranean; Black Sea ; Caspian Sea. Another subspecies in America. European subspecies migrates as far as S. Africa and west shores of Arabian Sea. North-western breeding group passes along coasts of France, Spain and Portugal, gives off element which passes into Mediterranean as far as Sicily ; and proceeds along west coast of Africa all the way to and round the Cape, some finishing their journey by travelling north as far as Natal.

MOVEMENTS. In Britain the normal coastal routes are used ; the east-south coast route ; the three west coast routes (W. Ireland, E. Ireland and W. England and Wales). Young of the year often travel a considerable distance *north* before they join normal autumnal southward stream. On east coast and south highly probable that many of the passengers are from Baltic and N. Sea as well as E. Britain. All are gone by winter.

TO READ. G. and A. Marples (1934). *Sea terns or sea swallows.* London. A. Landsborough Thomson (1943). *The migration of the Sandwich tern. Results of British ringing.* British Birds, vol. 37, pp. 62-9.

SANDWICH TERN, summer plumage, about 1/5 (for winter plumage see p. 182)

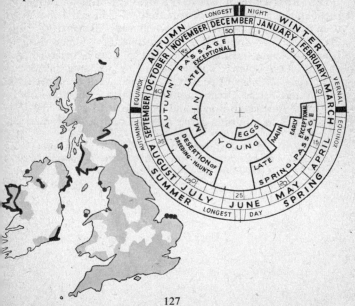

ROSEATE TERN *Sterna dougallii* MONTAGU 1813.

RECOGNITION. Small-medium. Length about 15 in. Wings not as long as Sandwich tern. Whiter appearance than common or arctic tern, from which also distinguished by very long tail streamers (and voice). Bill black with red at base in summer, also distinguishes from common or arctic tern as does pinkish-rose on breast in full breeding-plumage. Dives for fish in usual tern fashion. Mixes with other terns at all times. Call a hoarse " ach, ach " very easy to distinguish from other terns.

BREEDING. Social ; practically always in a minority in common or arctic (or other) tern colony and seems to share in flock-displays of other species. Own " pair " displays are of usual type. Little or no nest ; no lining. Eggs 1 to 3, normally 2, buff with reddish blobs and spots, length about $1\frac{3}{4}$ in. Both sexes incubate eggs 3 to $3\frac{1}{2}$ weeks and tend young probably for about 4 weeks. Nestling has curious " hairy " appearance which distinguishes it and nestling of Sandwich tern from those of other British breeding terns ; speckled grey-buff and dark brown, white under-parts. Young attains adult plumage in second summer after that in which it is hatched.

DISTRIBUTION AND MOVEMENTS. Has an extremely peculiar patchy breeding distribution. Chain starts in Caribbean ; Lesser Antilles — British Honduras — Bahamas — Florida — Bermuda — Virginia — Massachusetts — Maine — Sable Island — Azores — Britain — Tunisia (if it can be regarded as a chain). Also isolated colony belonging to same subspecies (*S. d. dougallii*) near Cape of Good Hope. Other subspecies in Indian and Pacific Oceans and Australasia. Migration along east coast America to Brazil, and west coast Africa to Cape. In Britain not half-a-dozen large colonies and seldom noted on migration.

TO READ. K. Williamson and M. N. and D. H. Rankin (1943). *Field notes on the breeding of the roseate tern* (Sterna d. dougalli *Mont.*). North-Western Naturalist, vol. 18, pp. 29-32.

ROSEATE TERN, summer plumage, about 1/4 (for winter plumage see p. 183)

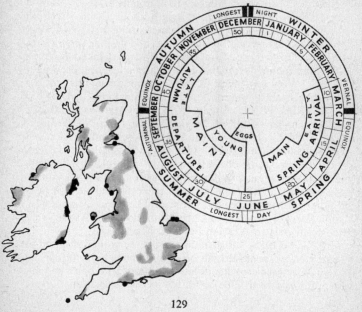

COMMON TERN *Sterna hirundo* LINNAEUS 1758.

RECOGNITION. Small-medium. Length up to 14 in. Wings not so long as Sandwich tern. Greyer than roseate tern, and tail-streamers do not normally extend beyond tips of folded wings. Black tip to red bill in summer distinguishes from arctic tern, as do relatively long legs, and accent, in alarm note " kee-ar," on *first* syllable. In winter has bill black with some red remaining at base (arctic tern totally black), but it is extremely difficult to tell juvenile or winter common and arctic terns apart (pp. 182-3); mistakes are likely. Flight light; wings beat through larger arc than roseate tern and between beats body sinks in typical tern fashion. Feeds by dropping from height into top foot of water, or by picking in flight from surface of water or land on fish (mostly sand-eels); also crustaceans, worms, echino-derms, molluscs and insects. Social at all times.

BREEDING. Social. Typical tern-type display with fish-flights, with or without fish, fish-presenting, gliding from heights, " slow-motion " flights ; on ground bowing, stretching, parad-ing, scraping. Many notes. Colonies on sand, shingle, marshes and flat rocks, often many miles inland. Nests simple hollows, sometimes lined grass. Eggs 2 to 4, usually 3, stone-colour with dark brown blobs and spots, length about 1½ in. Both sexes incubate eggs 3 to 4 weeks and manage young for about 4 weeks ; very occasional second broods. Eggs and nestling cannot be dis-tinguished from those of arctic tern. Young attains adult plumage in second summer after that in which it is hatched, occasionally in first. Very few breed in first or second summers, most for first time in third summer, and many not until fourth.

DISTRIBUTION. Chain of breeding-stations in America : Lesser Antilles—Gulf of Mexico—coast from N. Carolina to Gulf of St. Lawrence—Great Lakes—south end Hudson's Bay and Canadian lake system. Connects across Atlantic via Azores to European-Asiatic chain : on coasts and inland waters north to arctic circle and White Sea ; west to Britain ; south to Mediterranean and Tunisia ; east to Persia and western Asiatic Russia. Other subspecies in Tibet and E. Asia. Migrates down both coasts of America to Cape Horn, down W. Africa to Cape and from Asia to Arabian Sea and Madagascar.

MOVEMENTS. In Britain passage by normal east and west coast routes ; some British breeders moving *north* before going south. Overland crossing noted in autumn both north and south up and down river valleys. A few occasionally winter.

COMMON TERN, summer plumage, about 1/4 (for winter plumage see p. 182)

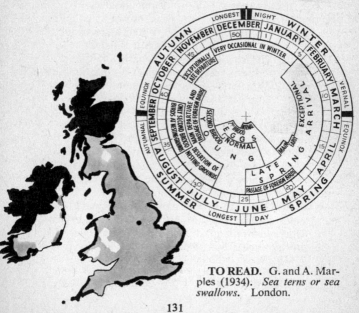

TO READ. G. and A. Marples (1934). *Sea terns or sea swallows*. London.

ARCTIC TERN *Sterna macrura* NAUMANN 1819.

RECOGNITION. Small-medium. Length up to 15 in. Wings not as long as Sandwich tern's. Greyer than roseate tern, and tail-streamers do not normally extend beyond tips of folded wings. Distinguished from common tern by bill, pure red in summer changing by stages to pure black in winter ; by legs, relatively short ; by voice, accent in alarm-note on *second* syllable of harsh " kee-ar." Extremely difficult to tell juvenile or winter arctic and common terns apart (pp. 182-3) and mistakes are to be expected. Flight and feeding-habits much as common tern's. Eats fish and insects ; in Arctic mainly crustaceans and molluscs, and some insects and fish. Social at all times.

BREEDING. Social. Displays as common tern. On breeding-grounds many notes the same as common tern's, but one like " kittiwake " has apparently only been heard in arctic tern colonies and may help in identification. Colonies in same sort of places as common tern though not as far inland. Nests simple hollows, sometimes lined grass. Eggs 1 to 4, normally 2, stone-colour boldly blotched dark brown, length $1\frac{1}{2}$ to $1\frac{3}{4}$ in. Both sexes incubate eggs for 3 weeks and manage young 3 to 4 weeks. Nestling downy ; not surely distinguishable from that of common tern ; grey-buff with dark brown spots and streaks, white under-parts (except throat). Young attains adult plumage in second summer after that in which it is hatched.

DISTRIBUTION. Breeds on all coasts and islands of Polar Basin, with extensions southwards, chief of these are : into east North Atlantic (Iceland—Faeroes—Britain—S.E. coasts North Sea—Baltic) ; up great arctic rivers of Siberia for a considerable distance ; into North Pacific as far as Aleutians and British Columbia ; up Mackenzie River to beyond Great Slave Lake ; into Hudson Bay ; down Labrador coast to Gulf of St. Lawrence and beyond to Massachusetts. Migrates along west coast of Europe and Africa, and along east and west coasts of America to Antarctic continent and Antarctic ocean where spends our winter (Antarctic summer) near the ice-limit.

MOVEMENTS. In Britain passage by normal east and west coast routes, swollen on east and south coasts by passengers from Baltic and continental North Sea coast. No evidence of northward movement before passage. No birds ever in winter.

TO READ. W. S. Bullough (1942). *Observations on the colonies of the arctic tern* (Sterna macrura *Naumann*) *on the Farne Islands.* Proceedings of the Zoological Society of London, series A, vol. 112, pp. 1-12.

ARCTIC TERN, summer plumage, about 1/4 (for winter plumage see p. 183)

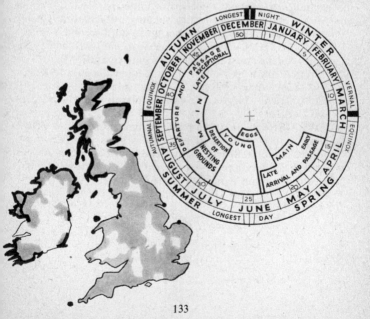

LITTLE TERN *Sterna albifrons* PALLAS 1764.

RECOGNITION. Small. Length about 9 in. Black cap; with white forehead in *summer* and winter (p. 182). Distinguished from winter black tern by absence of patch on white under-parts. Distinguished from winter arctic and common terns by smaller size, narrower wings, and yellow bill, legs and feet of adult (*dull* yellow in young). Flight as other terns, but wing-beats more rapid. Feeds in normal tern fashion, on crustaceans, worms, fish and molluscs. Frequently hawks for insects. Often individual and flocks tend to be small. Very fussy and noisy ; note " kwick-ick-ick, kreek-kik-ik " and, in dashing flight (not only on breeding-grounds) " twiri-didi-tiri-wiri."

BREEDING. Social. Displays as common tern but glides tend to be steeper and swifter. Butterfly-flight and fish-flights common. Colonies in Britain all coastal, on sands or shingle-banks ; nests scrape, occasionally lined grass. Eggs 2 to 4, normally 2, stone-colour with dark brown spots, length $1\frac{1}{4}$ to $1\frac{1}{2}$ in. Both sexes incubate eggs about 3 weeks and manage young about 4 weeks. Nestling has short down, pattern of brown mottling on sandy upper-parts, under-parts white. Young may attain adult plumage in first summer after that in which it is hatched, but sometimes does not do so until second.

DISTRIBUTION. The subspecies *S. a. albifrons* breeds, on coasts and inland, west to Britain, north to S. and E. Baltic (not into Arctic), south to N.W. Africa, Mediterranean and Persia, east to S.W. Asiatic Russia. Other subspecies Africa, E. Indies, America. Northern elements migrate south to a little beyond Equator.

MOVEMENTS. May be purely a summer visitor to Britain as there is no evidence that any of the birds breeding in W. Europe pass along British coast. Uses normal routes on east and west, as common tern, but no evidence of northward movement before autumn passage. None in winter.

TO READ. T. Lewis (1920). *Notes on the breeding-habits of the little tern.* British Birds, vol. 14, pp. 174-82. J. N. D. Smith (1921). *Notes on the little tern and young.* British Birds, vol. 15, pp. 50-6, and (1922). *On the nest-building of the little tern*, vol. 16, pp. 94-8.

LITTLE TERN, summer plumage, about 1/3 (for winter plumage see p. 182)

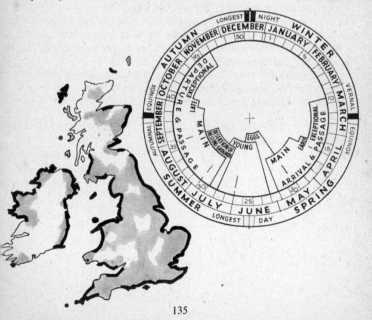

LITTLE GULL *Larus minutus* PALLAS 1776.

RECOGNITION. Small. Length about 11 in. Adult in summer has black head ; no black on wings but dark slaty under-sides ; bill red-brown, legs vermilion. In winter adult has head mostly white and very like black-headed gull's, but can be distinguished from it by dark slaty (as opposed to grey and white) undersides to wing and blackish (not red) bill ; also winter black-headed gull has black ends to upper-side of wing which *adult* winter little gull does not have. Immature little gull (p. 183) is at once distinguished from any stage of black-headed gull by black diagonal bar across upper-side of wings. Under-side of wings white, black tip to tail. Can be distinguished from immature kittiwake by head (dark crown, kittiwake has white crown with blackish ear-patch, back of head grey), bill (blackish, kittiwake has green), back (sooty barred with white, kittiwake's is spotted blackish with broad black band on back of neck). Flight more like tern's than gull's. Feeds by diving, picking from surface of water in flight, and hawking on fish, crustaceans, worms, molluscs and insects. Individual or small flocks. Voice " kek-kek-kek," or " kayee-kayee-kayee."

DISTRIBUTION AND MOVEMENTS. Breeds in Holland (one tiny, new colony), on south and east Baltic coasts and throughout European and Asiatic Russia, not north of the arctic circle. Migrates to the European shores of the Mediterranean and in Asia to mid-China. In Britain mainly passenger and winter visitor from south-western Baltic, mostly on east and south coast routes, a few W. England and Wales, rare Ireland and Scotland, occasional at inland lakes, reservoirs and sewage farms.

TO READ. Fr. Haverschmidt (1946). *Notes on the breeding of the little gull.* British Birds, vol. 39, pp. 14-18.

LITTLE GULL, summer plumage, about 3/10 (for immature plumage see p. 183)

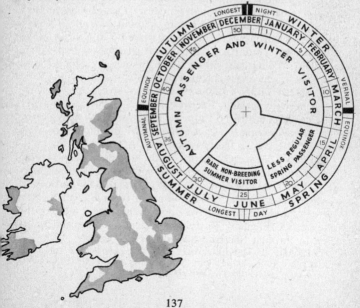

BLACK-HEADED GULL

Larus ridibundus (LINNAEUS) 1766.

RECOGNITION. Small-medium. Length about 15 in. Adult summer has brown head ; black tips and white front margin to wings ; bill and legs crimson. In winter (p. 184) adult has head mostly white and can be distinguished from common gull and kittiwake by red bill and legs and white front margin to wings. Immature b-h. g. also shows the white front margin to wings ; wings have black tips and dark mottling; crown is mottled brown, bill dull flesh, legs yellowish-flesh, back grey, black tip to tail : white under-parts distinguish it from imm. com. g. ; absence of black, diagonal band on upper-side wings distinguishes it from imm. k. or lit. g. Flight more tern-like than most gulls. Feeds by diving, picking, hawking, and probing mainly on fish, crustaceans, worms, molluscs, insects and other invertebrates, and on grain, seeds and garbage. Flocks, often large. Tame. Voice usually " kwup," other notes on breeding-grounds.

BREEDING. Social. Mutual courtship displays at colonies, in two main postures, very erect and very crouched ; latter used aggressively also. Female begs and male feeds her. Colonies by sea or inland, near water, on sand, shingle-banks, bogs and marshes ; nests of reeds and grasses. Eggs 2-4, normally 3, stone-buff spotted dark brown, length about 2 in. Both sexes incubate eggs 3 to $3\frac{1}{2}$ weeks and tend young 5 or 6 weeks. Nestling has bold pattern of dark brown patches on buff ; under-parts buff. Young may attain adult plumage in second summer after that in which it is hatched, but sometimes not until third.

DISTRIBUTION. *Larus r. ridibundus* breeds, on coasts and inland, west to Iceland, Faeroes, Britain and France, north to arctic circle, south to N. Italy, N. Balkans, Black Sea, east into Asia where becomes *L. r. sibiricus*. In Britain breeds widely inland. Migrates as far as Equator in Africa and Asia.

MOVEMENTS. Of British birds, about two-thirds simply disperse in autumn ; the rest move south, not often far ; small number to Iberian Peninsula, N.W. Africa and Azores mostly by west coast routes. Large numbers from E. and S. Baltic, Germany and Holland arrive on east coast, and most of these winter in S.E. England. Birds from Iceland, Faeroes and Norway come in through Shetland and down east coast.

TO READ. F. B. Kirkman (1937). *Bird behaviour.* London and Edinburgh. P. A. D. Hollom (1940). *Report on the 1938 survey of black-headed gull colonies.* British Birds, vol. 33, pp. 202-21, 230-44.

BLACK-HEADED GULL, summer plumage, about 1/5 (for winter plumage see p. 184)

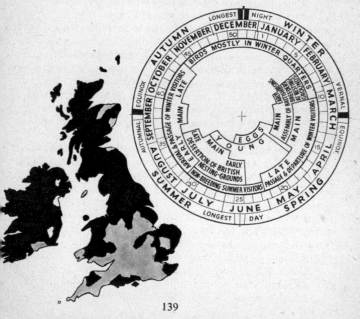

COMMON GULL *Larus canus* LINNAEUS 1758.

RECOGNITION. Medium. Length about 16 in. Adult has head white, in winter strongly streaked dusky brown; wings with black ends tipped with white; bill and legs yellow-green. Immature has black band at end of tail; head grey-brown streaked white, back brown, upper-side wings brown and grey with black-brown ends, no white at tips; under-sides of wing and body spotted and mottled brown; bill blackish and legs yellow flesh. Most likely to be confused with the very definitely larger herring gull, in both adult and immature plumage. H.g. has slower wing-beat and thicker bill; its wings, at rest, do not project so far beyond its tail. Its legs at all ages are flesh-coloured and are less yellow than those of the immature and less green than those of the adult c.g. Adult h.g.'s bill yellow with red spot; adult c.g.'s yellow-green, no red spot. The c.g.'s dark eye looks relatively large compared with that of the h.g. and its back is darker grey. Flight typically gull-style; more rapid wing-beats than larger gulls. Individual, and in flocks. Feeds by picking, probing, hawking, snatching, and occasionally diving on fish, crustaceans, worms, molluscs, insects; and roots and grain. Opens molluscs by dropping from height. Voice usually " kee-ah," other notes on breeding-grounds.

BREEDING. Social. Display includes much mutual courtship; false brooding, scraping, waddling, bowing with laughing note, begging and false feeding, raising head backwards. Colonies on rocky islands and shores, and on moors and bogs; nest built of stems or grass. Eggs 2-4, usually 3, olive with brown blotches, length about $2\frac{1}{4}$ in. Both sexes incubate eggs for about $3\frac{1}{2}$ weeks and manage young for 4 to 5 weeks. Nestling like black-headed gull's but darker marking on paler background. Young normally attains adult plumage in third summer after that in which it is hatched, but some may not do so until fourth.

DISTRIBUTION. *Larus canus canus* breeds in chain Faeroes —Scotland and N. and W. Ireland—Dungeness—Frisian Isles— Denmark—Baltic—Lapland. Migrates to the Mediterranean; breeds and winters inland as well as on coast. Other subspecies east of White Sea to E. Asia, and in western North America.

MOVEMENTS. Most British breeders move down east coast routes and inland; do not go very far except Highland breeders, of which many pass along outer west route to W. Ireland. Birds from Baltic and Frisian Isles arrive in autumn along England east coast, where joined from E. Scotland by birds which have come in through Shetland and Orkney.

COMMON GULL, summer plumage, about 1/5

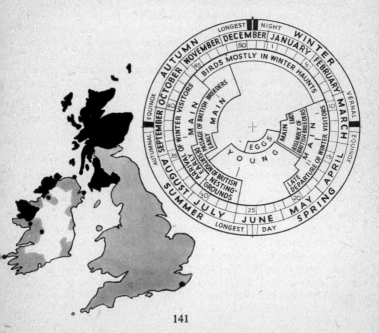

HERRING-GULL   *Larus argentatus* PONTOPPIDAN 1763.

RECOGNITION.   Medium-large.   Length about 22 in.   Adult
has white head, streaked with brown in winter ;   bill yellow with
red spot ;   mantle and wings grey, wings with black ends on
which white spots ;   tail and under-parts white.   Immature has
bill black, or black and yellow ;   plumage coarsely mottled with
brown, including head, tail and under-parts ;   ends of wings
sooty-brown to black ;   dark band near tip of tail.   Almost
impossible to distinguish yearling herring- and lesser black-
backed gulls in the field ;   though in the later stages immature
lesser black-backs tend to be darker, with browner tails.   For
comparison with common gull, see p. 140.   Flight steady and
direct, glides in typical gull fashion.   Usually in flocks, often
large.   Feeds by picking and probing ;   stamps on sand to bring
up worms ;   hawks, snatches, and sometimes dives ;   drops
molluscs from small height to break them.   Food includes fish,
crustaceans, worms, echinoderms, molluscs, insects, mammals
and birds.   A great scavenger, and part-time predator.   Voice
" k'yow-k'yow-k'yow," or " ki-och-ki-och-ki-och."

BREEDING.   Social.   Displays include grass-plucking, false
brooding, scraping, waddling, bowing with laughing note, begging and false feeding, raising head backwards, and communal
aerial dances.   Colonies typically on steep ground at top of cliffs
but may be on flat ground or even on islands in fresh-water lochs
not far from sea.   Nests lined quantities of vegetation, often seaweed.   Eggs 2-5, normally 3, olive-brown spotted dark brown,
length about $2\frac{3}{4}$ in.   Both sexes incubate eggs $3\frac{1}{2}$ to 4 weeks and
feed young about 6 weeks.   Nestling buff-grey spotted dark
brown, grey-white under-parts ;   indistinguishable from that of
lesser blackback.   Young normally attains adult plumage in
fourth summer after that in which it is hatched.

DISTRIBUTION.   *L. a. argentatus* breeds Faeroes, Britain,
N.W. France and continental North Sea coast to S. Norway.
Scandinavian h.g., *L. a. omissus*, darker mantle, yellow legs,
breeds W. Norway, Lapland, N. and E. Baltic, White Sea, and
has been recognized in autumn, winter and spring in Britain.
L. a. argentatus is not highly migratory, reaches Mediterranean.

MOVEMENTS.   British birds usually disperse and only
partially migrate, by coast routes.   Continental birds use east
coast route from Humber southwards, and many winter on east
and south coasts.   Frequent inland especially in hard weather.

TO READ.   F. Fraser Darling (1938).   *Bird flocks and the breeding
cycle . . .*   Cambridge.

HERRING GULL, summer plumage, about 1/7

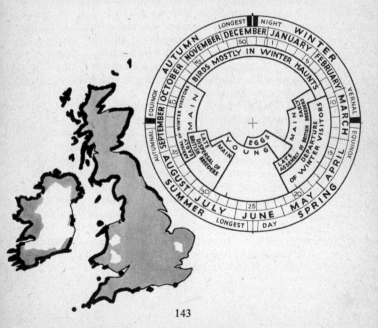

LESSER BLACK-BACKED GULL
Larus fuscus LINNAEUS 1758.

RECOGNITION. Medium-large. Length about 21 in. Adult differs from herring-gull (p. 142) by having mantle and wings dark slate-grey (British race) or black (Scandinavian race). Legs are yellow, not flesh-coloured, in adult. For distinction (if any) of immature, see p. 142. Differs from great black-back (which has black wings and mantle) by smaller size, less massive bill, and legs, which are whitish-flesh in great black-back. Flight much as herring-gull. Usually in flocks, often large; often with herring-gulls. Feeds mainly on fish, crustaceans, worms, molluscs, insects, mammals and birds; does not drop molluscs to break them, but is as great a scavenger, and a more aggressive and successful predator than herring-gull. Voice " ki-och, yoch-yoch-yoch," or like herring-gull's but deeper.

BREEDING. Social. Display of herring-gull pattern, includes false brooding, scraping, waddling, bowing, begging and false feeding, raising head backwards, and social aerial dances. Colonies often at tops of cliffs but not on steep ledges or on such steep slopes as herring-gull; often on quite low ground at sea level; much more often than herring-gull inland, quite usually on bare moors. Nest lined stems or seaweed. Eggs 2-4, usually 3, indistinguishable from herring-gull's. Both sexes incubate eggs 3½ to 4 weeks and feed young 4 to 5 weeks. Nestling indistinguishable from herring-gull's. Young normally attains adult plumage in fourth summer after that in which it is hatched; sometimes not until fifth.

DISTRIBUTION. *Larus fuscus graellsii*, the British lesser black-back, breeds in chain Iceland—Faeroes—Britain—Brittany—Channel Islands, and migrates to the W. Mediterranean and W. Africa as far as Equator. The Scandinavian lesser black-back, *L. f. fuscus*, breeds in Scandinavia, and the northern Baltic east to White Sea and Lake Onega, and migrates to E. Mediterranean, Persian Gulf, Red Sea, and African Great Lakes.

MOVEMENTS. British lesser black-back simply uses normal east and west coast routes; also passes extensively inland. A very few winter in S. England but to all intents and purposes a true summer visitor. Immature birds often summer some distance (south *or* north) from where they were hatched.

TO READ. A. Landsborough Thomson (1924). *The migrations of the herring-gull and lesser black-backed gull : results of the marking method.* British Birds, vol. 18, pp. 34-44.

LESSER BLACK-BACKED GULL, British, summer plumage, about 1/7 (for Scandinavian see p. 184)

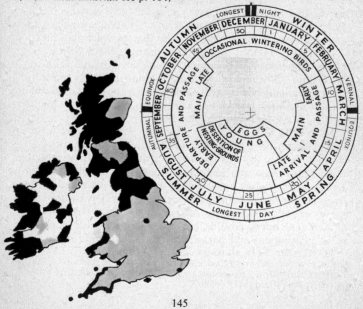

GREAT BLACK-BACKED GULL

Larus marinus LINNAEUS 1758.

RECOGNITION. Large. Length about 26 in. Mantle and wings black. Only a few dark streaks on head in winter. Bill massive. Legs whitish-flesh. Flight more ponderous and deliberate than lesser black-back's, with slower wing-beats. Immature may be distinguished from immature herring-gulls and lesser black-backs by size ; head, tail and under-parts are whiter ; pattern of mottling is more contrasted, and greater size and depth of bill stands out. More solitary and coastal than other gulls ; sometimes fair-sized flocks. Feeds by robbing, scavenging, hawking for insects, picking and probing ; and is the most successful predator of all the British gulls. Food includes crustaceans, worms, molluscs, echinoderms, insects, fish, birds and mammals. Voice a booming " yowk-owk-owk-owk."

BREEDING. Usually social. Display includes false brooding, scraping, bowing with laughing note and social aerial dances. Colonies on ledges and tops of cliffs and stacks, sometimes on moors some little distance from sea. Nest of stems, lined grass or seaweed. Eggs 2-5, usually 3, stone-colour with dark brown spots, length about 3 in. Both sexes incubate eggs $3\frac{1}{4}$ to 4 weeks and manage young for 7 to 8 weeks. Nestling like pale edition of lesser black-back's. Young normally attains adult plumage in fifth summer after that in which it is hatched.

DISTRIBUTION. Breeds in a chain : Nova Scotia—Gulf of St. Lawrence—Labrador—Greenland—Iceland—Faeroes— W. Britain—Normandy—Channel Islands—Brittany ; and west coast of Norway northwards along whole arctic coast of mainland Europe and Bear Island. In Europe migrates south to Mediterranean, Black Sea and Caspian Sea.

MOVEMENTS. Partial migrant. Immature birds probably migrate more often and further than adults ; more birds (from breeding stations in north) visit Britain in winter than leave it and large numbers winter from Wash to Thames-mouth. Usual east and west coast routes used ; rare overland. Many irregular movements in winter connected with weather or the movement of fishing boats. A large proportion of the winter population of all our large gulls, but particularly the great black-back, is semi-dependent and parasitic on the fishing industry.

TO READ. T. H. Harrisson and H. G. Hurrell (1933). *Numerical fluctuations of the great black-backed gull* (Larus marinus *Linn.*) *in England and Wales.* Proceedings of the Zoological Society of London, series A, vol. 103, pp. 191-209.

GREAT BLACK-BACKED GULL, summer plumage, about 1/8

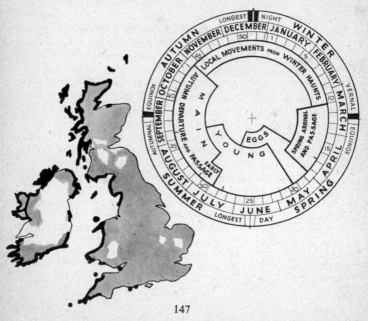

GLAUCOUS GULL

Larus hyperboreus GUNNERUS 1767.

RECOGNITION. Large. Length about 27 in. Adult has head white, streaked with brown in winter. Bill yellow with red spot. Legs flesh. Mantle and wings light grey ; no black on wings distinguishes from smaller adult herring-gull. Tail and under-parts white. Distinguished from the smaller Iceland gull by more massive bill, ring round eye lemon-yellow (brick-red in Iceland gull) and fact that in glaucous gull tips of folded wings *normally* extend not as far as, or no further than tip of tail, whereas in Iceland gull they extend beyond it. Immature glaucous gulls are like immature herring-gulls or lesser black-backs, only appreciably larger and finely and uniformly mottled ; and mottling extends to ends of wings and tail which are *not* sooty-black. Immature Iceland gulls can only be distinguished on size, size of bill, and position of wing-tips when wings folded, and errors are likely to arise. Habits as great black-back, flight with slow wing-beats (slower than Iceland gull) ; an even greater scavenger though not quite so bold a robber ; feeds on seaweed, berries, insects, worms, echinoderms, molluscs, crustaceans, fish, birds and mammals. Voice often rather high " heeee-yoch-h'yoch-och," and " kak-ak-ak."

DISTRIBUTION AND MOVEMENTS. Breeds all round the North Polar Basin on islands and arctic mainland (including Iceland), except in South Greenland where replaced by Iceland gull, with southward extensions into N. Pacific (Pribilov Islands), Hudson's Bay (to James Bay) and Labrador coast (to Newfoundland). In W. Europe migrates normally as far south as Britain and North Sea and occasionally pushes on as far as Iberian Peninsula and Atlantic Isles. In Britain winter visitors are regularly met with, most frequently in the north, along normal east coast route as far as Norfolk and along outer west coast route, Hebrides—W. Ireland. Most pass through Shetland where species quite common in autumn and winter. Inland only storm-driven.

TO READ. A. H. Paget Wilkes (1922). *On the breeding-habits of the glaucous gull as observed on Bear Island and in the Spitsbergen Archipelago.* British Birds, vol. 16, pp. 2-8.

GLAUCOUS GULL, summer plumage, about 1/8

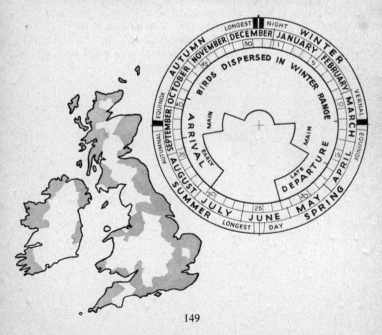

ICELAND GULL *Larus glaucoides* MEYER 1822.

RECOGNITION. Medium-large. Length about 21 in. Possibly should be regarded as subspecies of glaucous gull. Adult has head white, streaked with brown in winter. Bill yellow with red spot. Legs flesh. Mantle and wings light grey ; no black on wings distinguishes from adult herring-gull. Tail and under-parts white. Distinguished from larger glaucous gull by less massive bill, ring round eye brick-red (lemon-yellow in glaucous gull) ; in Iceland gull tips of wings extend beyond tail, in glaucous gull they normally do not do so. Immature Iceland gull distinguished from immature herring-gulls and lesser black-backs by fine uniform mottling and absence of sooty wing-ends and tail bar ; from immature glaucous gull often with difficulty on size, bill-size and position of folded wings. Habits as herring-gull ; wing-beats more rapid than glaucous gull. A part-time scavenger. Eats grain, berries, molluscs, crustaceans, fish, birds and mammals. Voice higher than herring - gull, " kee-orrh, korrh-korrh-korrh," and " ack-ack-ack."

DISTRIBUTION AND MOVEMENTS. Breeds only in South Greenland (seldom if ever in Iceland). Migrates to north-eastern U.S. ; in Europe to Iceland, Faeroes, Shetland and Norway, occasionally penetrating to North Sea and Baltic, N.W. Ireland and Channel. Beyond Shetland the rare British visitors are mostly found on the normal east coast and outer west coast routes. Inland only storm-driven.

ICELAND GULL, summer plumage, about 1/7

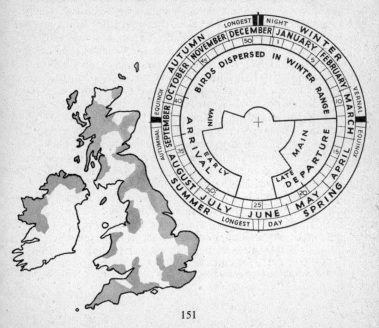

KITTIWAKE *Rissa tridactyla* (LINNAEUS) 1758.

RECOGNITION. Medium. Length about 16 in. Adult has head white, greyish in winter, with dark eye ; wings with pure black ends ; legs brown-black, bill yellow. Immature has a black diagonal bar across upper-side of wings ; head white with blackish ear-patch, back of head grey ; bill green, legs brown ; back spotted blackish with broad black band on back of neck. Flight light, swift and gliding ; quick wing-beat ; more active and at home in rough weather and seas than other British gulls. Solitary outside breeding-season. Feeds by diving from air or surface, or picking from in flight, or (very rare) picking from walk, on vegetable matter, molluscs, worms, insects, echinoderms, crustaceans, fish and mammals. Primarily a plankton-feeder. Voice "kitti-way-ake," other notes on breeding-grounds.

BREEDING. Social. Mutual " kittiwaking " courtship facing each other, bowing, head-raising, beak-scissoring, begging and feeding. Colonies usually on oceanic cliffs, exceptionally on ledges of harbour-warehouses (artificial " cliffs ") ; nest typically on tiny ledge or " pocket," built up as cup from available plant-stuff. Eggs 1-3, normally 2, stone-colour blotched brown, length about $2\frac{1}{4}$ in. Both parents incubate eggs about $4\frac{1}{2}$ weeks and manage young 4 to 5 weeks. Nestling silky white, grey-brown pattern on back and wings. Young normally attains adult plumage in third summer after that in which it is hatched.

DISTRIBUTION. *R. t. tridactyla* breeds in chain N. Greenland—Baffin Bay—Labrador—Gulf of St. Lawrence—Brittany —Sark—Britain—Faeroes—Iceland—E. Greenland—Norway and islands of coast of North Polar Basin, thence eastward to New Siberian Islands. Subspecies *R. t. pollicaris* breeds on arctic side of Bering Straits and into N. Pacific. In N. Atlantic *disperses* in all directions to oceans being limited in the north by the sea-ice and in the south by a temperature of about 68° F. (20° C.), seldom going south of the 60° F. isotherm (*i.e.*, south limit a line—not straight—roughly Florida to W. Africa).

MOVEMENTS. It is useless to think of British residents and winter visitors in terms of ordinary migration, or migration routes. In autumn there is a *dispersal* in the direction of the oceanic and offshore supplies of food, which resembles the movements of plankton-feeding fish such as herring.

TO READ. T. H. McKittrick, Jr. (1931). *Occurrence of kittiwakes on North Atlantic steamer routes.* Ibis, series 13, vol. 1, pp. 654-61.

KITTIWAKE, summer plumage, about 1/5 (for immature plumage see p. 185)

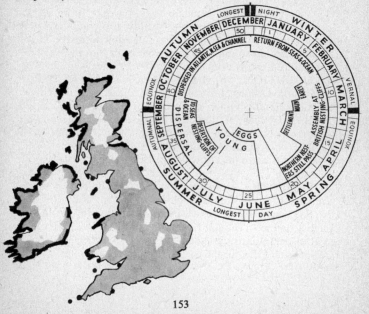

GREAT SKUA *Stercorarius skua* (BRÜNNICH) 1764.

RECOGNITION. Medium-large. Length about 2 ft. Uniform darkish brown with white patch in middle of leading edge of wing ; central tail feathers not elongated (tail looks short). Bill, legs and feet dull black. Much darker than immature gulls. In normal flight looks like a bulky, rather clumsy dark gull but shows great speed and powers of manoeuvre when chasing the birds it parasitises. Solitary outside breeding-grounds. Feeds by forcing other sea-birds (including gannets, gulls, terns and great shearwaters) to disgorge ; also scavenges, picks in flight from surface of water and may even dive ; and is a direct predator on birds and their young. Food list includes worms, molluscs, crustaceans, fish, birds and mammals. Usually silent outside breeding-grounds.

BREEDING. Semi-social. Usually have a meeting place somewhere accessible to members of loosely-knit colony where raise wings and utter growling " charr-charr-charr " in social display. Wing-raising also used by both sexes in courtship. Male throws head back and struts ; bowing also noted. Colonies on moorland near sea, nests are scrapes lined stems and grass. Eggs 1 or 2, usually 2, greyish with brown spots, length 2½ to 3 in. Both sexes incubate eggs 4 weeks or more and manage young for 6 or 7 weeks. Nestling brown, paler below. It is not known when young attains full adult plumage; it certainly does not do so until the third year after that in which it is hatched, and possibly does not do so until a later year.

DISTRIBUTION. *S. skua skua* breeds in Iceland, Faeroes, Shetland and Orkney, formerly in Caithness, and allegedly in South Greenland. Other subspecies in Antarctic and South Hemisphere. Northern subspecies disperses into Greenland Sea and northern N. Atlantic in summer, and in winter into North Sea and N. Atlantic as far south as 68° F. and usually no further than 60° F. isotherm (as kittiwake, p. 152, roughly a line Florida —W. Africa).

MOVEMENTS. From Shetland and Orkney birds pass into Atlantic in autumn, often through Hebrides, but also move into North Sea, where some spend winter, others moving south-west through Channel. Though this may ultimately be part of the general dispersal into the Atlantic it may also be regarded as a migration along the normal east and south coast routes.

TO READ. Frances Pitt (1922). *The great and arctic skuas in the Shetlands. Part I. The great skua.* British Birds, vol. 16, pp. 174-81.

GREAT SKUA, about 1/8

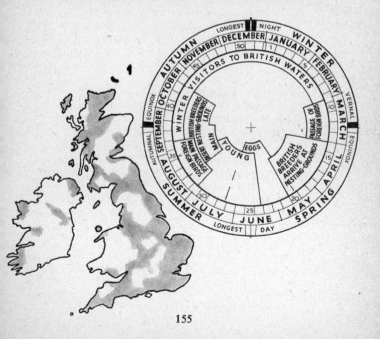

POMATORHINE SKUA

Stercorarius pomarinus (Temminck) 1815.

RECOGNITION. Medium. Length about 1½ ft.; central tail feathers project another 3 in. Larger and more robust than arctic or long-tailed skuas. Adult has central tail-feathers broad, blunt and *twisted*; two colour-phases, light and dark. Dark phase about 1 in 7 among British migrants. Light phase is blackish on crown and face, yellow over ears and back of neck, white throat and belly with sometimes brown band over breast, rest of plumage brown; in winter light areas from breast upwards barred brown and white and some white barring on upperparts. Dark form is of shade of great skua, almost uniform brown summer and winter. Immature birds of pale form have brown wings; head, neck and back barred brown and buff; underparts usually finely barred buff-white and very dark brown; and, at least in their first year, have central tail-feathers projecting only slightly beyond rest of tail; they are extremely difficult to distinguish in the field (as the size difference is not very great) from immature birds of the pale forms of the arctic and long-tailed skuas. Bill yellow brown with black tip, legs and feet dark. Flight steady, in style between gull and hawk, a bit heavier than arctic skua's. Feeds by forcing other sea-birds (includes large gulls, kittiwakes, terns) to disgorge, also scavenger, and direct predator on birds and small mammals (lemmings). Voice "which-yew." Individual outside breeding-grounds.

DISTRIBUTION AND MOVEMENTS. Breeds round the Polar Basin in Novaya Zemlya and on the arctic mainland coast from the White Sea to Bering Straits, in N. Alaska, the Canadian arctic archipelago and W. Greenland. In autumn leaves Polar Basin into N. Atlantic and through Bering Straits into Pacific. In Atlantic winters in much the same regions as kittiwake (see p. 152) which it chiefly parasitises, and may pass to them through Shetland and Orkney, thence through North Sea and Channel or through Hebrides to open ocean. On return in spring does *not* appear to use south and east coast routes but is sometimes seen passing through Hebrides.

TO READ. H. N. Southern (1944). *Dimorphism in* Stercorarius pomarinus (*Temminck*). Ibis, vol. 86, pp. 1-16.

POMATORHINE SKUA, light phase, summer plumage, about 1/6

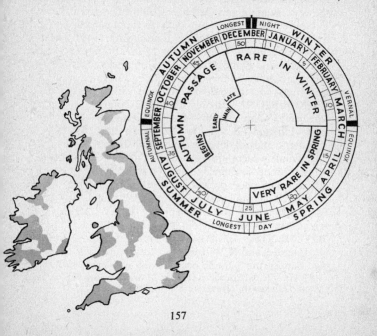

ARCTIC SKUA *Stercorarius parasiticus* (LINNAEUS) 1758.

RECOGNITION. Medium. Length about 15 in ; central tail-feathers project another 3 in. Smaller than pomatorhine but larger than long-tailed skua. Adult has central feathers of tail narrow and pointed, not twisted. Small white wing-patch. Two colour-phases, similar to p. skua's save yellow over ears and neck not so intense or widespread in light phase. Always has some dark on breast usually amounting to dark band. Dark phase about 5 in 6 among British breeders. For difficulty in distinguishing immature skuas, see p. 156. Bill darker than p. skua's ; legs dark. Flight swift and direct, in style between Sandwich tern's and hawk's. Feeds by forcing other sea-birds (includes *Larus* gulls, kittiwakes, terns and auks) to disgorge ; may co-operate with another of same species ; also scavenger, fishes by diving, and direct predator on birds and small mammals (especially on breeding-grounds). Food list includes crustaceans, molluscs, insects, fish, mammals, birds and plants. Voice " kiaow." Sometimes social outside breeding-grounds.

BREEDING. Social ; sometimes solitary. " Switchback " display flight with skids and tumbling ; mutual wing-lifting and bowing, begging and feeding. Colonies on moors near sea, or on tundra ; birds use hummocks as standing places. Nest a depression lined grass or stems. Eggs 1 to 3, usually 2, olive-brown spotted brown, length about $2\frac{1}{4}$ in. Both sexes incubate $3\frac{1}{2}$ to 4 weeks and manage young 3 to $5\frac{1}{2}$ weeks. Nestling silky, dark brown, lighter underneath. Young does not attain adult plumage until fourth year after that in which it is hatched.

DISTRIBUTION. Breeds all round Polar Basin in chain : E. Greenland—Jan Mayen—Iceland—Faeroes—N. Britain—Norway—Lapland—N. Baltic—European and Asiatic arctic coast, tundra and all large islands (Spitsbergen to E.)—Commander Islands—Aleutians—Alaska—Yukon—Canadian North-West and arctic archipelago—N. Labrador—W. Greenland. Spends winter in open oceans, but passes to its objectives more along normal coastal routes than other skuas. In Atlantic spends winter mostly in S. hemisphere, off S.W. Africa ; others winter in Arabian Sea and off New Zealand and S. America.

MOVEMENTS. Birds pass to Atlantic by east and south coasts, Hebrides and N.W. Ireland. Autumn passage much more marked than spring. Some occasionally winter in North Sea.

TO READ. H. N. Southern (1943). *The two phases of* Stercorarius parasiticus (*Linnaeus*). Ibis, vol. 85, pp. 443-85.

ARCTIC SKUA, light phase, summer plumage, about 1/6

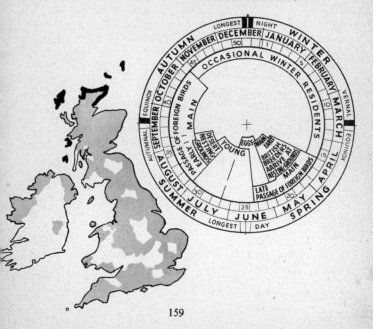

LONG-TAILED SKUA

Stercorarius longicaudus VIEILLOT 1819.

RECOGNITION. Small-medium. Length about 14 in. ; central tail-feathers add up to 8 in. to this. Smaller than arctic skua. Adult has very long slender middle tail-feathers. Dark phase is exceptionally rare. Normal light phase bird has same coloration as arctic skua, except that in summer it never has any dark patches or band on breast. For difficulty in distinguishing immature pomatorhine, arctic and long-tailed skuas, see under first-named, p. 156. Bill black, as opposed to pomatorhine and arctic skuas, legs grey, feet black. Flight swift and graceful, in style between arctic tern's and hawk's. Feeds at sea by forcing terns and gulls to disgorge. Breeds normally, apparently, only where lemmings are available on which preys direct ; also hawks for insects. Does not usually attempt to hawk small birds as do other skuas. Food list includes berries, worms, crustaceans, insects, fish, birds and mammals. Not much of a scavenger. Usually silent away from breeding-grounds. Often social, usually in small parties.

DISTRIBUTION AND MOVEMENTS. Breeds round Polar Basin in chain : N.E. Greenland—Jan Mayen—Norway—Lapland—White Sea—Novaya Zemlya—European and Asiatic arctic coasts to Bering Straits—N. American arctic coasts and tundra (including Mackenzie)—Southampton Island—N. Labrador peninsula—Canadian arctic archipelago—N.W. Greenland. Disappears in winter into Atlantic and E. Pacific, but exactly where it goes, or what species (if any) it parasitises in its winter range, is not known. On passage to this unknown objective some birds, presumably from European Arctic, pass through North Sea and appear at various places in Britain along east and south coastal routes ; a few others filter through Hebrides and N.W. Ireland. Practically none pass through Britain in spring.

LONG-TAILED SKUA, light phase, summer plumage, about 1/6

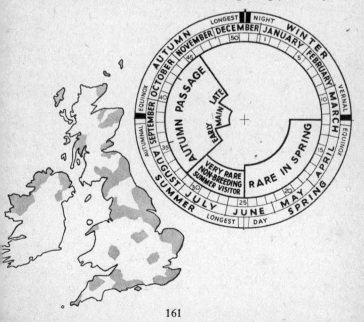

RAZORBILL   *Alca torda* LINNAEUS 1758.

RECOGNITION. Medium. Length about 16 in. Adult in summer has black head and upper-parts, white under-parts ; in winter white on throat and neck. Young birds have dark brown instead of black. Adults have deep laterally compressed bill, black, crossed by nearly vertical line which is white in summer ; this line absent in young birds, which have less deep bill and might be confused with guillemots. Mouth yellow inside. Black legs and feet. Normally very rapid wing-beats ; does not glide or soar, but beats wings slowly when flying down from cliffs. Patters surface of water before taking off. When pursued likely to dive. Swims rapidly under water with wings, can submerge for $\frac{3}{4}$ minute, hunts fish (particularly sand-eels), planktonic and bottom-living crustaceans, worms and molluscs. Voice a low continuous growling, seldom heard away from breeding-cliffs. Social.

BREEDING. Social. Courtship display usually mutual, head raising and scissoring ; also social displays with swimming games on water. Single egg laid (no nest) occasionally on flat cliff-ledges, but usually in crevices, sheltered pocket ledges, broken rocks, talus slopes or even rabbit burrows at tops or bottoms of sea cliffs. Very occasionally 2 eggs, light brown, spotted dark brown (but variable), length about 3 in. Both parents incubate for 4 to 5 weeks; young flutters to sea 2 or 3 weeks after hatching and is joined by one or both of its parents. Nestling is mostly brown-black, its down being tipped with white. Young gets adult plumage in second year after that in which it is hatched.

DISTRIBUTION. Breeds in a chain : Bay of Fundy—Gulf of St. Lawrence—Newfoundland—Labrador—W. Greenland—Iceland—Faeroes—Britain—Brittany—Channel Is.—Heligoland—Norway—Bear Island—Lapland—White Sea—Baltic (Gulf of Bothnia—Gottland—Bornholm). That part of chain between Faeroes and Channel Is. is *Alca torda britannica*, the British razorbill ; rest *A. t. torda*. E. Atlantic element winters south to Bay of Biscay, Portugal and through Straits into W. Mediterranean. Autumn movements constitute more a *dispersal* than migration.

MOVEMENTS. In autumn northern British birds mostly move north and east, into North Sea and mouth of Baltic ; some go hundreds of miles further north up coast of Norway. Birds from south Britain may also go north or east, but mostly go to Bay of Biscay or W. Mediterranean. Inland only storm-driven.

TO READ. R. Perry (1940). *Lundy, isle of puffins*, London, pp. 111-47.

RAZORBILL, summer plumage, about 1/5

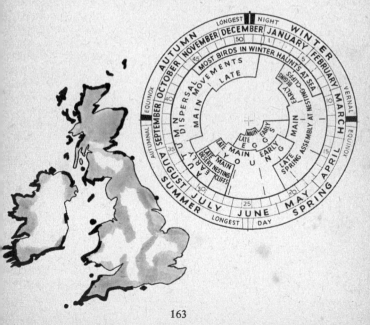

GREAT AUK   *Alca impennis* LINNAEUS 1758.

RECOGNITION. Extinct. Length about 2½ ft. Very like double-length razorbill with ordinary razorbill's wings. Powerful deep grooved bill, black. Legs and feet black. Very dark brown head and upper-parts ; under-parts white. In winter white on throat. Oval white patch in front of eye. Inside of mouth orange. Swam rapidly on surface in same attitude as razorbill, and with wings under water extremely rapidly and powerfully. Fed on fish and crustaceans. Quite incapable of flight. Voice has been described as low croak but of a captured bird it has been written " it used to make a great noise, like that made by a gannet, but much louder, when shutting its mouth," and of others " when they are being killed they squeak like pigs." Apparently often in pairs or small parties outside breeding-season. About 80 skins exist.

BREEDING. Social. Display unknown. Colonies on low rocky islands and skerries on to which birds could struggle and waddle at any state of the tide. Single egg, greenish-white spotted dark brown, length about 5 in., value of good specimen over £300 ; about 75 blown specimens exist. Probably both sexes shared in incubation during May and June; share of sexes in management of young not known. Combined incubation and fledging periods possibly 6 or 7 weeks. Nestling and age of maturity unknown.

DISTRIBUTION AND MOVEMENTS. Breeding range used to be some or all of the following stations, and probably others : Gulf of St. Lawrence : Cape Breton (? breeding *c.* 1593)—Bird Rocks, Magdalen Islands (raided 1534)—Penguin Island, South Newfoundland (raided 1536 and probably again 1578)—Funk Island, East Newfoundland (raided 1534 and probably again before 1555, last known raid 1794). Greenland : Graahs Is., off S.E. coast (? breeding *c.* 1652). Iceland : Geirfuglasker off C. Reykjanes (raid 1808, big raid 1813, island submerged by volcanic disturbance 1830)—Eldey, 8 miles nearer C. Reykjanes (last great auks of all, 1844)—Geirfuglasker in Westmann Is. (possibly breeding before 1800). Faeroes (possibly breeding before 1800). Britain : Papa Westray in Orkney (female killed probably on egg ; male lived in cave for some time after but shot by W. Foulis in 1813)—St. Kilda group (used to breed, possibly still breeding 1697, probably no longer breeding 1758, one captured Hirta 1821, last British bird caught Stac an Armin in or about 1840 and beaten to death by

GREAT AUK, summer plumage, about 1/10

L. M'Kinnon and D. MacQueen as thought to be witch)—Calf of Man (? breeding *c.* 1652). One captured Waterford, Ireland, 1834.

When the great auk flourished it seems to have dispersed on the west side of the Atlantic from Disco, W. Greenland normally to Cape Cod and exceptionally to Florida, and on the east side from Norway to Bay of Biscay and (perhaps exceptionally) to Gibraltar.

The final extinction of the great auk, after 300 years of slaughter by seamen for food, was almost certainly on Eldey, Iceland, on 4 June, 1844, when two adults and an egg were found. S. Islefsson killed one adult, J. Brandsson the other (they were male and female) and K. Ketilson, finding the egg cracked, destroyed it.

TO READ. Symington Grieve (1885). *The great auk, or garefowl* (Alca impennis, *Linn.*), *its history, archaeology, and remains.* London and Edinburgh. A. F. R. Wollaston (1921). *Life of Alfred Newton.* London, pp. 27-52. James Fisher (1945). *Alfred Newton and the auk.* Bird Notes and News, vol. 21, pp. 75-7.

GUILLEMOT   *Uria aalge* (PONTOPPIDAN) 1763.

RECOGNITION.   Medium.   Length about 16 in.   Adult in summer has brown head and upper-parts, white under-parts ; in winter white on throat and neck and ear-coverts ; dark line extends back from eye across white.   In the " bridled guillemot " white ring embraces eye from which white line runs back across head.   This form less than 1 per cent. of population breeding S. Britain but numbers increase with latitude; in Shetland quarter of breeding population.   Young birds very like adults.   Tapering, sharp-pointed black bill, yellow inside (more orange than razorbill's) ;   legs and feet yellow-brown.   Flight and swimming powers as razorbill ;   can stay under over a minute, hunts fish (particularly sand-eels), crustaceans, worms and molluscs.   Voice growling but more variable than razorbill's ; has been written " gwoo-err."   Quiet at sea.   Generally social.

BREEDING.   Social.   Bowing, head raising, scissoring, false preening, begging and feeding all part of mutual courtship display;   also water games.   Single egg laid (no nest) on flat cliff-ledge or stack-top;   highly variable ground colour and spots. Both sexes incubate 4 to 7 weeks, and young flutters to sea 2 to 3 weeks after hatching.   Parents, or one parent, accompany young on water for some time.   Nestling has coarse white down on head, neck and throat, rest brownish.   Young practically attains adult plumage in first season after that in which it is hatched.

DISTRIBUTION.   Breeds in chain : Nova Scotia—Gulf of St. Lawrence—Labrador—S. Greenland—Iceland—Faeroes— Highland Scotland (*U. a. aalgae*); rest of Britain—Brittany— N.W. Spain—Berlengas (off Portugal)—Heligoland (*U. a. albionis*);   Baltic (*U. a. intermedia*) ;   Norway—Bear Island— Novaya Zemlya (*U. a. hyperborea*).   Other subspecies in N. Pacific.   N. Atlantic guillemots disperse in winter, reach Cape Cod on W. and Canaries on E., also penetrate into Mediterranean as far as Italy.

MOVEMENTS.   Dispersal of British birds not fully worked out but some from N. Britain certainly move north, or north-east to Norway, in autumn.   Along east coast route a normal autumn and spring movement.   Inland only storm-driven.

TO READ. H. N. Southern and E. C. R. Reeve (1942). *The common guillemot* (Uria aalge *Pont.*). Proceedings of the Zoological Society of London, series A, vol. 111, pp. 255-76.

GUILLEMOT, summer plumage, about 1/5

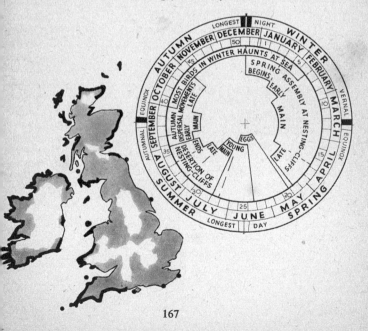

BLACK GUILLEMOT *Uria grylle* (LINNAEUS) 1758.

RECOGNITION. Small-medium. Length about 13 in. Adult in summer black except for large white patch on wing ; mainly white in winter with pronounced blackish mottling on back and neck. Bill black, pointed, and red inside ; legs and feet red. Flight rapid and low, direct, takes off from water by pattering. Submerges and swims under water with wings and feet ; stays under up to 1¼ minutes, hunts small fish and bottom-living crustaceans, molluscs and worms. Voice a plaintive, high-pitched whine, " tystie, tystie," usually heard near breeding-grounds. Solitary on feeding-grounds.

    BREEDING. Individual or only semi-social. Displays concern pair (swimming round opening beak, false drinking, bowing) and small social groups (follow-my-leader on water and in air, diving together). Bond between mated pairs is still observable during social water games. Groups or individuals breed on rocky or cliffy coasts or islands (cliffs need not be high), in crevices, cracks, under broken rocks, in talus slopes, or in old rabbit burrows. No nest. Eggs 1 to 3, normally 2, whitish with dark brown and grey; length about 2¼ in. Both sexes incubate eggs 3 to 4 weeks and manage young in hole for about 5 weeks. Nestling very dark brown, paler below. Young attains adult plumage in second summer after that in which it is hatched.

    DISTRIBUTION AND MOVEMENTS. Black guillemot, *U. g. grylle*, breeds in chain : Bay of Fundy—Gulf of St. Lawrence—S. Labrador—Iceland—Faeroes—N.W. Britain—mouth of Baltic—Norway—Lapland coast—White Sea—Gulf of Bothnia—Central Baltic. Arctic black guillemot, or Mandt's guillemot, *U. g. mandtii*, breeds all round Polar Basin in chain: E. Greenland—Jan Mayen—Bear Island—Spitsbergen—Franz Josef Land—Novaya Zemlya—Siberian coasts and islands—Alaska—Canadian arctic coasts and islands—Hudson's Bay—Baffin Island—W. and S. Greenland—Labrador S. to Hamilton R. Northern birds move south but general dispersal of species in winter does not extend south limit of distribution very far beyond its position in summer. In U.S. reaches Cape Cod, in Europe disperses in North Sea. Keeps in sight of coast. In Britain breeding birds are very sedentary and usually spend winter near breeding-places ; the birds seen occasionally on east coast in winter are probably from northern Europe.

    TO READ. Edward A. Armstrong (1940). *Birds of the grey wind.* London, etc., pp. 202-13.

BLACK GUILLEMOT, summer plumage, about 1/5

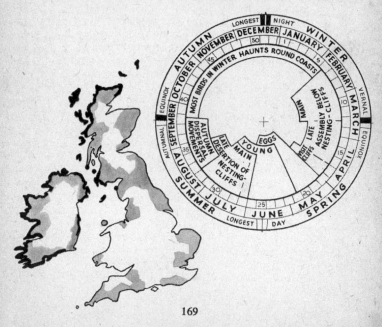

LITTLE AUK *Alle alle* (LINNAEUS) 1758.

RECOGNITION. Small. Length about 8 in. Dumpy bird with very short, black bill. Black upper-parts, white under-parts, legs and feet brown-black. Usually met with in Britain in winter plumage, when has white ear-coverts and throat ; in summer whole head, neck, throat and top half of breast is deep chocolate. Flight direct but rather fussy, with very rapid wing-beats ; does not patter over water to take off. Flocks near breeding-grounds often vast and perform evolutions. Usually scattered individuals in winter oceanic range. Swims under water with wings and feet, normally submerges up to half a minute ; feeds mainly on planktonic crustaceans, also eats bottom-living crustaceans, worms, molluscs, fish and algae. Voice on breeding-grounds a loud, piercing and continuous chatter but silent usually in winter quarters.

DISTRIBUTION AND MOVEMENTS. Breeds in chain : Iceland (Grimsey)—Jan Mayen—Bear Island—Spitsbergen—N. Greenland—Franz Josef Land—Novaya Zemlya. Disperses in winter into south Greenland Sea and North Atlantic. Normal limit is not far beyond limit of sea-ice, which brings it to Newfoundland Banks, Iceland, Faeroes and near Norwegian coast, but only irregularly to Britain. In some winters, however, goes much further south in numbers, reaching West Indies and actually entering western Mediterranean. Inland in Britain only storm-driven, but has managed to get so stranded in nearly every county.

LITTLE AUK, winter plumage; about 3/8

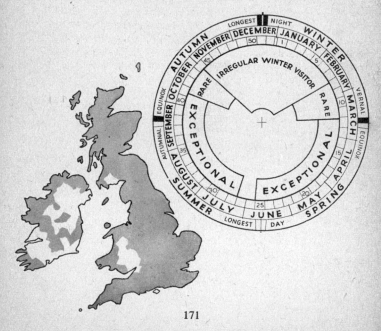

PUFFIN *Fratercula arctica* (LINNAEUS) 1758.

PUFFIN, summer plumage, about 1/5

RECOGNITION. Small-medium. Length about a foot. Triangular, parrot-like grooved bill (blue, yellow and red in summer, brown and orange in winter) ; black upper-parts, light grey face, white under-parts. Legs and feet red in summer, yellow in winter. Mouth yellow inside. Young much as adults but bill is very much smaller and less deep and not grooved. In winter bill of adult is intermediate in size between that of young and summer adult as outside of base of summer bill is shed (including horny yellow rim at base, yellow " bit " at angle of mouth). Also shed is blue horny triangle above eye and narrow rectangle below eye. Flight of usual auk type, low with very rapid wing-beats. Pitches clumsily and patters surface of water to take off. When pursued dives rather than fly. Swims under water with wings ; submerges for half a minute or more ; eats fish, planktonic and bottom-living crustaceans and molluscs. Voice usually on breeding-grounds but sometimes on sea, " parr-harr-harr," a growl, rather low. Social at all times.

BREEDING. Social. In mutual courtship display on land pair face each other and scissor bills together. On water swim round each other. Also bowing used in courtship and as threat. Colonies often vast, on grass slopes on, below or above cliffs, often on grass-covered rocky islands. Eggs laid in crevices in rocks or talus slopes, or in burrows excavated by birds themselves, rabbits or Manx shearwaters. Egg 1, very occasionally 2, whitish, often marked brown, length about 2½ in. Female mostly, but occasionally male, incubates egg about 6 weeks ; both parents feed young in burrow about 6 weeks ; young remains up to a week in burrow by itself, then walks (fluttering down steeps) to sea by night, being unable yet to fly. Nestling very downy, uniform brown with white on belly. Young gets full adult plumage in third season after that in which it is hatched.

DISTRIBUTION AND MOVEMENTS. Breeds in chain: Bay of Fundy—Gulf of St. Lawrence—Labrador to Ungava Bay —Greenland—Jan Mayen—Iceland—Faeroes—Britain—Channel Islands—Brittany—Berlengas off Portugal; mouth of Baltic—Norway—Lapland coast—Bear Island—Spitsbergen— Novaya Zemlya. From Faeroes to S. Norway inclusive is *F. a. grabae*; in Spitsbergen is *F. a. naumanni*; rest is *F. a. arctica*. In winter northern birds are driven south by ice and dispersal generally takes a wide form; on the east side of the Atlantic birds reach the Canaries and normally penetrate the Mediterranean as far as the Adriatic; on the west they reach the Delaware. Although in general puffins keep to offshore waters within the hundred-fathom line, two birds ringed at St. Kilda reached Newfoundland in their first year. Some British breeders certainly disperse to north-east across North Sea. Birds hatched in one place may breed a hundred miles away. Inland only storm-driven.

TO READ. R. M. Lockley (1934). *On the breeding-habits of the puffin* : . . . British Birds, vol. 27, pp. 214-23.

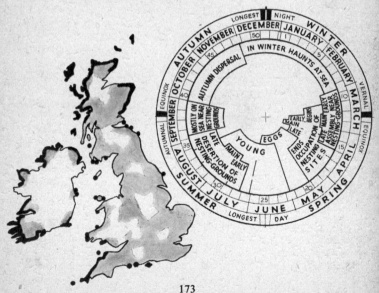

FIELD IDENTIFICATION IN GENERAL.

The following principles are compiled from the published advice of H. G. Alexander, B. W. Tucker (the present editor of *British Birds*) and the late H. F. Witherby (editor of *The Handbook of British Birds* and previous editor of *British Birds*).

Faced with a problem of field identification make notes and sketches AT ONCE. Do not attempt to use this, or any other book, or any field key, until you have made *full* notes on *all* the bird's plumage. Otherwise the book may suggest things to you that you did not see or hear.

Be precise about the exact parts of a bird's surface. These have definite names, which are fairly simple, and can be memorised. See diagram on p. 14.

Note—Distance from bird.

Whether using glasses.

Conditions and direction of light.

General characters and behaviour at rest.

General characters and behaviour in flight.

Habitat.

Whether alone or with birds of same or other species.

Colour, size and shape of bill, legs and feet.

Precise size, shape and *position* of what appear to you to be distinctive markings.

Shape of wing and coloration (noté colour, extent and *position* of bars, if any).

Shape, length of tail and coloration of tail and rump (extent and *position* of bars, if any).

Voice.

Date, time.

Initials of companions in case subsequent confirmation is needed.

There is every advantage in writing down your notes as comparisons with the characteristics of species with which you are familiar—as long as you really *are* familiar with them. The pictures that follow are intended to help with such comparisons ; with the exception of the plate of gulls all are in winter plumage.

TO READ. H. F. Witherby (1930). *Sight records*. British Birds, vol. 23, pp. 343-4. H. G. Alexander (1944). *On field identification of birds*: British Birds, vol. 38, pp. 89-93. With particular reference to this book, B. W. Tucker (1940). *General field-characteristics of waders*. in *The handbook of British birds*, ed. H. F. Witherby and others, London, vol. 4, pp. 153-4. As a warning, B. W. Tucker (1942). *The Berkhamsted grey shrike*. British Birds, vol. 36, pp. 51-3.

BLACK-TAILED
GODWIT

BAR-TAILED
GODWIT

KNOT

RED-NECKED
PHALAROPE

GREY
PHALAROPE

SANDERLING

TEMMINCK'S
STINT

LITTLE
STINT

DUNLIN

CURLEW-
SANDPIPER

COMMON
SANDPIPER

PURPLE
SANDPIPER

REEVE

GREEN
SANDPIPER

WOOD-
SANDPIPER

GREENSHANK

REDSHANK

SPOTTED
REDSHANK

RINGED
PLOVER

KENTISH
PLOVER

LITTLE
RINGED PLOVER

GREY
PLOVER

GOLDEN
PLOVER

SANDWICH TERN

COMMON TERN

LITTLE TERN

ARCTIC TERN

ROSEATE TERN

LITTLE GULL
(IMMATURE)

LESSER
BLACKBACK

BLACK-
HEADED
GULL
(WINTER)

GREAT
BLACKBACK

FULMAR

COMMON
GULL

ICELAND
GULL

KITTIWAKE

GLAUCOUS
GULL

KITTIWAKE
(IMMATURE)

HERRING-
GULL

EXTREME RARITIES

THE following is the list of those species of sea-birds and waders which have been seen or obtained in Britain, but which are so rare that they have not, in my opinion, merited any full mention. Their *Handbook* numbers, and (in brackets) the number of times the *Handbook* records them as having been observed, are given. Only the great snipe has been recorded more than 100 times.

W442-3 American and Asiatic golden plovers, *Pluvialis dominica* (17 or 18).

W352 Madeiran fork-tailed petrel, *Oceanodroma castro* (4).

W353 Wilson's petrel, *Oceanites oceanicus* (about 12).

W354 Frigate-petrel, *Pelagodroma marina* (2).

W357-8 Little shearwater, *Puffinus assimilis* (11).

W359 Audubon's shearwater, *Puffinus l'herminieri* (1).

W361-2 Mediterranean and North Atlantic shearwaters, *Puffinus kuhlii* (2)

W364 Kermadec petrel, *Pterodroma neglecta* (1).

W365 Capped petrel, *Pterodroma hasitata* (1).

W366 Collared petrel, *Pterodroma leucoptera* (1).

W367 Bulwer's petrel, *Bulweria bulwerii* (7).

W369 Black-browed albatross, *Diomedea melanophrys* (1).

W390 Eskimo curlew, *Numenius borealis* (7 or 8).

W391 Slender-billed curlew, *Numenius tenuirostris* (about 6).

W392 Bartram's sandpiper, *Bartramia longicauda* (about 13).

W394 Great snipe, *Capella media*, tiny trickle in autumn of passengers S. E. England, elsewhere probably under a hundred records (see opp., p. 187).

W399 Red-breasted snipe, *Limnodromus griseus* (25 or 26).

W408 American stint, *Calidris minutilla* (4).

W410 Semi-palmated sandpiper, *Calidris pusilla* (1).

W411 American pectoral sandpiper, *Calidris melanotos* (64).

W412 Siberian pectoral sandpiper, *Calidris acuminata* (4).

W413 Baird's sandpiper, *Calidris bairdii* (5).

W414 Bonaparte's sandpiper, *Calidris fuscicollis* (about 15).

W418 Buff-breasted sandpiper, *Tryngites subruficollis* (19).

W419 Broad-billed sandpiper, *Limicola falcinellus* (20).

W420 Terek sandpiper, *Xenus cinereus* (7).

W422 Spotted sandpiper, *Actitis macularia* (8 or 9).

W425 Solitary sandpiper, *Tringa solitaria* (8).

W426 Yellowshank, *Tringa flavipes* (13).

W427 Greater yellowshank, *Tringa melanoleuca* (5).

W433 Marsh-sandpiper, *Tringa stagnatilis* (8 or 9).

W434 Grey-rumped sandpiper, *Heteroscelus incanus* (2).
W445 Caspian plover, *Eupoda asiatica* (4 or 5).
W447 Killdeer plover, *Oxyechus vociferus* (12 or 13).
W448 Sociable plover, *Chettusia gregaria* (7).
W453 Cream-coloured courser, *Cursorius cursor* (about 27).
W454 Pratincole, *Glareola pratincola* (about 38).
W455 Black-winged pratincole, *Glareola nordmanni* (10).
W460 Macqueen's bustard, *Chlamydotis undulata* (4).
W463 Whiskered tern, *Chlidonias hybrida* (22).
W464 White-winged black tern, *Chlidonias leucopterus* (under
W465 Gull-billed tern, *Gelochelidon nilotica* (over 40). [100).
W466 Caspian tern, *Hydroprogne caspia* (over 30).
W472 Sooty tern, *Sterna fuscata* (10 or more).
W473 Bridled tern, *Sterna anaethetus* (1).
W474 Sabine's gull, *Xema sabini* (under 100).
W475 Ross's gull, *Rhodostethia rosea* (2).
W476 Bonaparte's gull, *Larus philadelphia* (7).
W479 Mediterranean black-headed gull, *Larus melano-
cephalus* (10 or more).
W480 Great black-headed gull, *Larus ichthyäetus* (6).
W490 Ivory gull, *Pagophila eburnea* (about 70).
W500 Brünnich's guillemot, *Uria lomvia* (about 15).

GREAT SNIPE, about 1/4

The least rare of these extreme rarities. Length about 9 in., bill
another 2¼ in. Breeds from Baltic and Scandinavia east into
Asia. Larger and darker than common snipe. Rises silent or with
grunt, without twisting and showing much white on sides of tail. But
very hard to tell from common snipe whose individuals vary in size,
plumage and behaviour.

INDEX

Albatross, Black-browed   *p.* 186
American golden plover..   186
—— pectoral sand-
    piper   ..   186
—— stint   186
Arctic skua   ..   158–9
—— tern   ..   132–3
Asiatic golden plover   ..   186
Audubon's shearwater   ..   186
Auk, Great   164–5
——, Little   170–1
Avocet   112–3

Baird's sandpiper   ..   186
Bar-tailed godwit..   ..   48–9
Bartram's sandpiper   ..   186
Black guillemot   ..   168–9
—— tern   ..   124–5
—— ——, White-winged   187
Black-backed gull, Great   146–7
—— ——, Lesser   144–5
Black-browed albatross   ..   186
Black-headed gull   138–9
—— —— ——, Great   187
—— —— ——, Medi-
    terranean   187
Black-tailed godwit   ..   50–1
Black-winged pratincole..   187
—— stilt   ..   110–1
Bonaparte's gull   ..   187
—— sandpiper   ..   186
Bridled tern   187
Broad-billed sandpiper   186
Brünnich's guillemot   ..   187
Buff-breasted sandpiper   186
Bulwer's petrel   186
Bustard, Great   ..   118–9
——, Little   ..   120–1
——, Macqueen's   ..   187

Capped petrel   186
Caspian plover   187
—— tern   187
Collared petrel   ..   186
Common gull   ..   140–1
—— sandpiper   ..   84–5
—— tern   ..   130–1
Cormorant   31–3
Courser, Cream-coloured   187

Crane   ..   ..   *p.* 122–3
Cream-coloured courser..   187
Curlew   52–3
——, Eskimo   186
——, Slender-billed   ..   186
——, Stone-   ..   116–7
Curlew-sandpiper   ..   72–3

Dotterel   106–7
Dunlin   70–1

Eskimo curlew   186

Fork-tailed petrel, Leach's   38–9
—— —— ——, Madeiran   186
Frigate-petrel   186
Fulmar   45–7

Gannet   34–5
Glaucous gull   ..   148–9
Godwit, Bar-tailed   ..   48–9
——, Black-tailed   ..   50–1
Golden plover   ..   102–4
—— ——, American   186
—— ——, Asiatic   ..   186
Great auk   164–5
—— bustard   ..   118–9
—— black-backed gull..   146–7
—— black-headed gull..   187
—— shearwater..   ..   42–4
—— skua   154–5
—— snipe   186–7
Greater yellowshank   ..   186
Green sandpiper   ..   88–9
Greenshank   94–5
Grey phalarope   ..   62–3
—— plover   ..   104–6
Grey-rumped sandpiper   187
Guillemot   ..   166–7
——, Black   ..   168–9
——, Brünnich's   ..   187
Gull, Black-headed   138–9
——, Bonaparte's   187
——, Common   ..   140–1
——, Glaucous   ..   148–9
——, Great black-backed   146–7
——, Great black-headed   187
——, Herring-   ..   142–3
——, Iceland   ..   150–1
——, Ivory-   187

Gull, Lesser black-backed
      p. 144–5
——, Little 136–7
——, Mediterranean black-
  headed 187
——, Ross's 187
——, Sabine's 187
Gull-billed tern 187

Herring-gull 142–3

Iceland gull 150–1
Ivory-gull 187

Jack snipe 60–1

Kentish plover 100–1
Kermadec petrel 186
Killdeer plover 187
Kittiwake 152–3
Knot 68–9

Lapwing 108–9
Leach's fork-tailed petrel 38–9
Lesser black-backed gull 144–5
Little auk 170–1
—— bustard 120–1
—— gull 136–7
—— ringed plover .. 98–9
—— shearwater 186
—— stint.. 74–5
—— tern 134–5
Long-tailed skua 160–1

Macqueen's bustard .. 187
Madeiran fork-tailed petrel 186
Manx shearwater.. .. 40–1
Marsh-sandpiper .. 186
Mediterranean black-
  headed gull 187
  —— shearwater 186

North Atlantic shearwater 186

Oystercatcher 114–5

Pectoral sandpiper, Ameri-
     can.. 186
  —— ——, Siber-
     ian .. 186
Petrel, Bulwer's 186
——, Capped 186
——, Collared 186
——, Frigate- 186
——, Fulmar 45–7

Petrel, Kermadec .. *p.* 186
——, Leach's fork-tailed 38–9
——, Madeiran fork-
  tailed `..` .. 186
——, Storm- 36–7
——, Wilson's 186
Phalarope, Grey .. 62–3
 ——, Red-necked .. 64–5
Plover, American golden 186
——, Asiatic golden .. 18
——, Caspian 187
——, Golden 102–4
——, Grey 104–5
——, Kentish 100–1
——, Killdeer 187
——, Little ringed .. 98–9
——, Ringed 96–7
——, Sociable 187
Pomatorhine skua .. 156–7
Pratincole 187
 ——, Black-winged 187
Puffin 172–3
Purple sandpiper .. 78–9

Razorbill 162–3
Red-breasted snipe .. 186
Red-necked phalarope .. 64–5
Redshank 90–1
 ——, Spotted .. 92–3
Ringed plover 96–7
 —— ——, Little .. 98–9
Roseate tern 128–9
Ross's gull 187
Ruff 82–3

Sabine's gull 187
Sanderling 80–1
Sandpiper, American pec-
    toral 186
—— , Baird's .. 186
—— , Bartram's .. 186
—— , Bonaparte's .. 186
—— , Broad-billed .. 186
—— , Buff-breasted 186
—— , Common .. 84–5
—— , Curlew- .. 72–3
—— , Green .. 88–9
—— , Grey-rumped 187
—— , Marsh- .. 186
—— , Purple .. 78–9
—— , Semi-palmated 186
—— , Siberian pec-
   toral .. 186
—— , Solitary .. 186

Sandpiper, Spotted .. *p.* 186
—— , Terek .. 186
—— , Wood- .. 86–7
Sandwich tern 126–7
Semi-palmated sandpiper 186
Shag 31–3
Shearwater, Audubon's .. 186
—— , Great .. 42–4
—— , Little .. 186
—— , Manx .. 40–1
—— , Mediterranean 186
—— , North Atlantic 186
—— , Sooty .. 43–4
Siberian pectoral sand-
piper 186
Skua, Arctic .. 158–9
—— , Great .. 154–5
—— , Long-tailed .. 160–1
—— , Pomatorhine .. 156–7
Slender-billed curlew .. 186
Snipe 58–9
—— , Great .. 186–7
—— , Jack .. 60–1
—— , Red-breasted .. 186
Sociable plover 187
Solitary sandpiper .. 186
Sooty shearwater .. 43–4
—— tern.. .. 187
Spotted redshank .. 92–3
Spotted sandpiper .. 186
Stilt, Black-winged .. 110–1

Stint, American .. .. *p.* 186
——, Little 74–5
——, Temminck's .. 76–7
Stone-curlew 116–7
Storm-petrel 36–7

Temminck's stint .. 76–7
Terek sandpiper .. 186
Tern, Arctic 132–3
——, Black 124–5
——, Bridled 187
——, Caspian 187
——, Common 130–1
——, Gull-billed 187
——, Little 134–5
——, Roseate 128–9
——, Sandwich 126–7
——, Sooty 187
——, Whiskered 187
——, White-winged black 187
Turnstone 66–7

Whimbrel 54–5
Whiskered tern 187
White-winged black tern 187
Wilson's petrel 186
Woodcock 56–7
Wood-sandpiper 86–7

Yellowshank 186
—— , Greater .. 186

To Hon. Secretary
The British Trust for Ornithology
c/o The Zoological Society of London
Regent's Park, n.w.8

Having read James Fisher's *Bird Recognition*, vol. 1, I would like to join the British Trust for Ornithology, and enclose a subscription (the Trust asks its members to pay 10*s*. a year, or more if they can).

I am interested in the Trust and would like some literature about it.

Name . . . .
(MR., MRS., MISS, ETC.)

Address . . . .

. . . .

. . . . *Date* . . . .

**PLEASE WRITE IN BLOCK CAPITALS, AND CROSS
OUT WHAT DOES NOT APPLY**